Accounting
Teacher's Guide

CONTENTS

Curriculum Overview   1

Accounting LIFEPAC Management   2

Special Instructions for Accounting 10

Answer Keys:

    LIFEPAC 1 13

    LIFEPAC 2 22

    LIFEPAC 3 44

    LIFEPAC 4 59

    LIFEPAC 5 97

    LIFEPAC 6 108

    LIFEPAC 7 124

    LIFEPAC 8 155

    LIFEPAC 9 161

    LIFEPAC 10 183

Self Test Keys 205

LIFEPAC Test Keys 243

Editors: Alan Christopherson, M.S.

Jennifer L. Davis, B.S.

Alpha Omega Publications ®

300 North McKemy Avenue, Chandler, Arizona 85226-2618
© MM by Alpha Omega Publications, Inc.   All rights reserved.
LIFEPAC is a registered trademark of Alpha Omega Publications, Inc.

Accounting

ACCOUNTING OVERVIEW
- Careers in Accounting
- Nature of Bookkeeping & Accounting
- Types of Business Ownership
- The Basic Accounting Equation
- Changes in the Accounting Equation

STARTING AN ACCOUNTING SYSTEM
- Creating a Chart of Accounts
- Accounting Concepts & Practices
- The Balance Sheet, General Journal & General Ledger
- Recording & Posting Opening Entry

ANALYZING & JOURNALIZING TRANSACTIONS
- Using the T Account
- Transactions Affecting Balance Sheet & Income Statement Items
- Transaction Analysis & Journal Entries

POSTING TO THE GENERAL LEDGER
- Types of Ledger Accounts
- The Expanded Chart of Accounts
- Opening the Ledger & Posting Journal Entries
- Preparing a Trial Balance

PREPARING THE WORKSHEET
- The Six-Column Worksheet
- The Eight-Column Worksheet
- Adjustments on a Worksheet
- Calculating Net Income/Net Loss
- Review Worksheet Procedures

FINANCIAL STATEMENTS FOR A PROPRIETORSHIP
- Income Statement
- Statement of Owner's Equity
- The Balance Sheet

RECORDING & POSTING THE ADJUSTING & CLOSING ENTRIES
- Adjusting Entries
- Closing Entries
- Prepare a Post-Closing Trial Balance

PAYROLL RECORDS
- Payroll Functions & Deductions
- Calculating Employee Earnings
- Completing the Payroll Register
- Payroll Records & Methods

PAYROLL ACCOUNTING, TAXES, REPORTS
- Recording a Payroll
- Recording Employer's Payroll Taxes
- Reporting Taxes
- Payment of Taxes

BUSINESS SIMULATION REINFORCEMENT ACTIVITY
- Purpose
- Materials Required
- Steps to Complete
- Review all Materials

LIFEPAC 1 · LIFEPAC 2 · LIFEPAC 3 · LIFEPAC 4 · LIFEPAC 5 · LIFEPAC 6 · LIFEPAC 7 · LIFEPAC 8 · LIFEPAC 9 · LIFEPAC 10

STRUCTURE OF THE LIFEPAC CURRICULUM

The LIFEPAC curriculum is conveniently structured to provide one teacher handbook containing teacher support material with answer keys and ten student worktexts for each subject at grade levels two through twelve. The worktext format of the LIFEPACs allows the student to read the textual information and complete workbook activities all in the same booklet. The easy to follow LIFEPAC numbering system lists the grade as the first number(s) and the last two digits as the number of the series. For example, the Language Arts LIFEPAC at the 6th grade level, 5th book in the series would be LA 605.

Each LIFEPAC is divided into 3 to 5 sections and begins with an introduction or overview of the booklet as well as a series of specific learning objectives to give a purpose to the study of the LIFEPAC. The introduction and objectives are followed by a vocabulary section which may be found at the beginning of each section at the lower levels, at the beginning of the LIFEPAC in the middle grades, or in the glossary at the high school level. The student should learn all vocabulary words before working the LIFEPAC sections to improve comprehension, retention, and reading skills.

Each activity or written assignment has a number for easy identification, such as 1.1. The first number corresponds to the LIFEPAC section and the number to the right of the decimal is the number of the activity.

Teacher/Adult checkpoints, which are essential to maintain quality learning, are found at various locations throughout the LIFEPAC. The teacher should check: 1) neatness of work and penmanship, 2) quality of understanding (tested with a short oral quiz), 3) thoroughness of answers (complete sentences and paragraphs, correct spelling, etc.), 4) completion of activities (no blank spaces), and 5) accuracy of answers as compared to the answer key (all answers correct).

The self test questions are also number coded for easy reference. For example, 2.015 means that this is the 15th question in the self test of Section II. The first number corresponds to the LIFEPAC section, the zero indicates that it is a self test question, and the number to the right of the zero the question number.

The LIFEPAC Test is packaged at the centerfold of each LIFEPAC. It should be removed and put aside before giving the booklet to the student for study.

Answer and test keys have the same numbering system as the LIFEPACs and appear at the back of this handbook. The student may be given access to the answer keys (not the test keys) under teacher supervision so that he can score his own work.

A thorough study of the Curriculum Overview by the teacher before instruction begins is essential to the success of the student. The teacher should become familiar with expected skill mastery and understand how these grade level skills fit into the overall skill development of the curriculum. The teacher should also preview the objectives that appear at the beginning of each LIFEPAC for additional preparation and planning.

TEST SCORING and GRADING

Answer keys and test keys give examples of correct answers. They convey the idea, but the student may use many ways to express a correct answer. **The teacher should check for the essence of the answer, not for the exact wording.** Many questions are high level and require thinking and creativity on the part of the student. Each answer should be scored based on whether or not the main idea written by the student matches the model example. "Any Order" or "Either Order" in a key indicates that no particular order is necessary to be correct.

Most self tests and LIFEPAC Tests at the lower elementary levels are scored at 1 point per answer; however, the upper levels may have a point system awarding 2 to 5 points for various answers or questions. Further, the total test points will vary; they may not always equal 100 points. They may be 78, 85, 100, 105, etc.

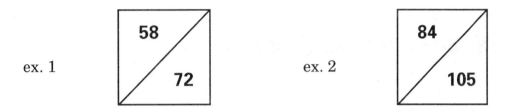

ex. 1   58 / 72   ex. 2   84 / 105

A score box similar to ex.1 above is located at the end of each self test and on the front of the LIFEPAC Test. The bottom score, 72, represents the total number of points possible on the test. The upper score, 58, represents the number of points your student will need to receive an 80% or passing grade. If you wish to establish the exact percentage that your student has achieved, find the total points of his correct answers and divide it by the bottom number (in this case 72.) For example, if your student has a point total of 65, divide 65 by 72 for a grade of 90%. Referring to ex. 2, on a test with a total of 105 possible points, the student would have to receive a minimum of 84 correct points for an 80% or passing grade. If your student has received 93 points, simply divide the 93 by 105 for a percentage grade of 89%. Students who receive a score below 80% should review the LIFEPAC and retest.

The following is a guideline to assign letter grades for completed LIFEPACs based on a maximum total score of 100 points.

LIFEPAC Test   =   60% of the Total Score (or percent grade)
Self Test   =   25% of the Total Score (average percent of self tests)
Reports   =   10% or 10* points per LIFEPAC
Oral Work   =   5% or 5* points per LIFEPAC
*Determined by the teacher's subjective evaluation of the student's daily work.

Example:

LIFEPAC Test Score	= 92%	92 x .60	=	55	points
Self Test Average	= 90%	90 x .25	=	23	points
Reports			=	8	points
Oral Work			=	4	points

TOTAL POINTS   =   90 points

Grade Scale based on point system:

100	–	94	=	A
93	–	86	=	B
85	–	77	=	C
76	–	70	=	D
Below		70	=	F

TEACHER HINTS and STUDYING TECHNIQUES

LIFEPAC Activities are written to check the level of understanding of the preceding text. The student may look back to the text as necessary to complete these activities; however, a student should never attempt to do the activities without reading (studying) the text first. Self tests and LIFEPAC Tests are never open-book tests.

Writing complete answers (paragraphs) to some questions is an integral part of the LIFEPAC Curriculum in all subjects. This builds communication and organization skills, increases understanding and retention of ideas, and helps enforce good penmanship. Complete sentences should be encouraged for this type of activity. Obviously, single words or phrases do not meet the intent of the activity, since multiple lines are given for the response.

Review is essential to student success. Time invested in review where review is suggested will be time saved in correcting errors later. Self tests, unlike the section activities, are closed book. This procedure helps to identify weaknesses before they become too great to overcome. Certain objectives from self tests are cumulative and test previous sections; therefore, good preparation for a self test must include all material studied up to that testing point.

The following procedure checklist has been found to be successful in developing good study habits in the LIFEPAC curriculum.

1. Read the Introduction and Table of Contents.

2. Read the objectives.

3. Recite and study the entire vocabulary (glossary) list.

4. Study each section as follows:

      a. Read all the text for the entire section, but answer none of the activities.

b. Return to the beginning of the section and memorize each vocabulary word and definition.

c. Reread the section, complete the activities, check the answers with the answer key, correct all errors, and have the teacher check.

d. Read the self test but do not answer the questions.

e. Go to the beginning of the first section and reread the text and answers to the activities up to the self test you have not yet done.

f. Answer the questions to the self test without looking back.

g. Have the self test checked by the teacher.

h. Correct the self test and have the teacher check the corrections.

i. Repeat steps a–h for each section.

5. Use the SQ3R* method to prepare for the LIFEPAC Test.

6. Take the LIFEPAC Test as a closed book test.

7. LIFEPAC Tests are administered and scored under direct teacher supervision. Students who receive scores below 80% should review the LIFEPAC using the SQ3R* study method and retake the test.

*SQ3R: Scan the whole LIFEPAC.
Question yourself on the objectives.
Read the whole LIFEPAC again.
Recite through an oral examination.
Review weak areas.

GOAL SETTING and SCHEDULES

Basically, two factors need to be considered when assigning work to a student in the LIFEPAC curriculum.

The first factor is time. An average of 45 minutes should be devoted to each subject, each day. Remember, this is only an average. Because of extenuating circumstances a student may spend only 15 minutes on a subject one day and the next day spend 90 minutes on the same subject.

The second factor is the number of pages to be worked in each subject. A single LIFEPAC is designed to take 3 to 4 weeks to complete. Allowing about 3-4 days for LIFEPAC introduction, review, and tests, the student has approximately 15 days to complete the LIFEPAC pages. Simply take the number of pages in the LIFEPAC, divide it by 15 and you will have the number of pages that must be completed on a daily basis to keep the student on schedule. For example, a LIFEPAC containing 45 pages will require 3 completed pages per day. Again, this is only an average. While working a 45 page LIFEPAC, the student may complete only 1 page the first day if the text has a lot of activities or reports, but go on to complete 5 pages the next day.

FORMS

The sample weekly lesson plan and student grading sheet forms are included in this section as teacher support materials and may be duplicated at the convenience of the teacher.

The student grading sheet is provided for those who desire to follow the suggested guidelines for assignment of letter grades found on page 4 of this section. The student's self test scores should be posted as percentage grades. When the LIFEPAC is completed the teacher should average the self test grades, multiply the average by .25 and post the points in the box marked self test points. The LIFEPAC percentage grade should be multiplied by .60 and posted. Next, the teacher should award and post points for written reports and oral work. A report may be any type of written work assigned to the student whether it is a LIFEPAC or additional learning activity. Oral work includes the student's ability to respond orally to questions which may or may not be related to LIFEPAC activities or any type of oral report assigned by the teacher. The points may then be totaled and a final grade entered along with the date that the LIFEPAC was completed.

The Student Record Book, which was specifically designed for use with the Alpha Omega curriculum, provides space to record weekly progress for one student over a nine-week period as well as a place to post self test and LIFEPAC scores. The Student Record Books are available through the current Alpha Omega catalog; however, unlike the enclosed forms these books are not for duplication and should be purchased in sets of four to cover a full academic year.

WEEKLY LESSON PLANNER			
			Week of:

	Subject	Subject	Subject	Subject
Monday				
	Subject	Subject	Subject	Subject
Tuesday				
	Subject	Subject	Subject	Subject
Wednesday				
	Subject	Subject	Subject	Subject
Thursday				
	Subject	Subject	Subject	Subject
Friday				

WEEKLY LESSON PLANNER

Week of:

	Subject	Subject	Subject	Subject
Monday				
Tuesday	Subject	Subject	Subject	Subject
Wednesday	Subject	Subject	Subject	Subject
Thursday	Subject	Subject	Subject	Subject
Friday	Subject	Subject	Subject	Subject

Student Name _____   Year _____

LP #	Self Test Scores by Sections 1	2	3	4	5	Self Test Points	LIFEPAC Test	Oral Points	Report Points	Final Grade	Date
01											
02											
03											
04											
05											
06											
07											
08											
09											
10											

LP #	Self Test Scores by Sections 1	2	3	4	5	Self Test Points	LIFEPAC Test	Oral Points	Report Points	Final Grade	Date
01											
02											
03											
04											
05											
06											
07											
08											
09											
10											

LP #	Self Test Scores by Sections 1	2	3	4	5	Self Test Points	LIFEPAC Test	Oral Points	Report Points	Final Grade	Date
01											
02											
03											
04											
05											
06											
07											
08											
09											
10											

Special Instructions for Accounting

WELCOME to this exciting new curriculum offering from Alpha Omega Publications. Accounting systems play a significant role in every modern business. It is the method of finding the universal measurement of the success or failure of a business often referred to as *the bottom line*. Accurate accounting information is essential in directing the decision making process that enables a business to succeed in a competitive business environment. These same basic principles can be applied to maintain personal financial records.

Here are some tips that should help your student successfully complete this course:

1. This program teaches accounting procedures and assumes that the student has already mastered basic mathematical skills. Therefore, all computations should be done with a calculator.

2. Use a calculator that has large buttons and a display that is easy to read. The calculator on a computer could also be used.

4. 10-key adding machine skills are not discussed in this material but could be made an optional requirement.

3. Drill and review the vocabulary words. They are key to understanding both the information as it is presented and the instructions for the activities.

4. Many of the LIFEPACs include extra blank forms. These can be duplicated and used as they are needed.

5. It is highly recommended that most students complete the *optional activities for extra credit* that are in the final section of many of the LIFEPACs.

6. Often an early mistake can affect several accounting forms. In some situations it might be best to grade one form before the student completes the next one.

7. It is important that each form be completed as neatly and as completely as possible. Have students observe the proper error correction procedures.

8. For illustration purposes, the answer keys show the year on all dates as (20—). However, students should always use the complete current year: 2001, 2002, 2003, etc.

9. It is important that students achieve a high level of mastery for each accounting procedure as it is presented. The final unit of the program program utilizes most of the procedures learned throughout the year in completing a business simulation.

10. Take a field trip to observe the accounting department in a medium to large business.

IMPORTANT NOTES:

The **Teacher's Notes** that appear throughout this Teacher's Guide usually contain grading instructions; however, they may also give suggestions for instruction or clarification of concepts presented. It is recommended that you preview the appropriate section of the Teacher's Guide before assigning the work to the student.

LIFEPAC 10 is a business simulation that represents a complete accounting cycle. To ensure that the student starts and continues correctly, the project should be completed under your supervision. The work must be neat and legible, and corrections should follow the procedures discussed in previous LIFEPACs. Normally, work of this type is done in pen with the exception of the worksheet; however, you may feel that using a pencil is a better way to complete this project. NOTE: Students may use previous LIFEPACs for reference while completing this simulation.

ANSWER KEYS

VOCABULARY

Accountant – a person responsible for interpreting financial data.

Asset – anything of value that is owned.

Basic accounting equation – a formula that illustrates the relationship between assets, liabilities and capital.

Bookkeeper – a person responsible for recording business transactions.

Business entity – the existence of a business as an artificial individual.

Business transaction – business activity that causes changes in the value of assets, liabilities and capital.

Capital – the financial interest of the owner of a business; determined by subtracting total liabilities from the total assets. Also called Owner's Equity.

Corporation – an association of individuals united for a common purpose to use a common name and to change members without dissolving the association; a business chartered under state law and owned by stockholders.

Drawing – an owner's withdrawal of cash from his business for personal use.

Equities – the claims against the assets of a business.

Fiscal period – the period of time that the books are open to record transactions and summarize accounting information.

Liability – any amount that is owned.

Partnership – an association of two or more persons to carry on as co-owners of a business for profit.

Proprietor – the owner of a business.

Revenue – the increase in owner's equity caused by income from the sale of goods and services.

Sole proprietorship – a business owned and managed by one person.

SECTION I (see Self Test 1)

SECTION II (see Self Test 2)

SECTION III

								Accounts Affected	Account Classification	Change in Balance

3.1 A = $130

3.2 C = $120

3.3 L = $70

	Assets	= Liabilities	+	Capital
3.4	$8,000	= $2,000	+	**$6,000**
3.5	**$6,000**	= $3,200	+	$2,800
3.6	$2,500	= **$600**	+	$1,900
3.7	**$3,600**	= $1,800	+	$1,800

3.8 A

3.9 C

3.10 A

3.11 A

3.12 L

3.13 A

3.14 L

		Accounts Affected	Account Classification	Change in Balance
				Either order:
3.15	a.	Cash	Asset	Increase
	b.	Capital	Capital	Increase
3.16	a.	Cash	Asset	Increase
	b.	Capital	Capital	Increase
3.17	a.	Cash	Asset	Decrease
	b.	Capital	Capital	Decrease
3.18	a.	Cash	Asset	Decrease
	b.	Capital	Capital	Decrease
3.19	a.	Supplies	Asset	Increase
	b.	Cash	Asset	Decrease
3.20	a.	Prepaid Ins.	Asset	Increase
	b.	Accts. Payable	Liability	Increase

SECTION IV

4.1 a. asset
 b. liability
 c. asset
 d. asset
 e. liability
 f. asset
 g. capital
 h. liability
 i. asset
 j. capital
 k. asset

4.2 a. no change
 b. decrease
 c. no change
 d. increase
 e. no change
 f. increase
 g. decrease

4.3

	Assets	= Liabilities	+ Capital
a.	increase	no effect	increase
b.	no effect	no effect	no effect
c.	increase	no effect	increase
d.	increase	increase	no effect
e.	decrease	no effect	decrease
f.	decrease	decrease	no effect
g.	decrease	no effect	decrease

		Accounts Affected	Account Classification	Change in Balance
		Either order:		
4.4	1.	Cash	Asset	Increase
		Capital	Capital	Increase
	2.	Equipment	Asset	Increase
		Cash	Asset	Decrease
	3.	Capital	Capital	Decrease
		Cash	Asset	Decrease
	4.	Equipment	Asset	Increase
		Accts. Payable	Liability	Increase
	5.	Cash	Asset	Increase
		Capital	Capital	Increase
	6.	Cash	Asset	Increase
		Capital	Capital	Increase
	7.	Supplies	Asset	Increase
		Cash	Asset	Decrease
	8.	Cash	Asset	Decrease
		Capital	Capital	Decrease
	9.	Accts. Payable	Liability	Decrease
		Cash	Asset	Decrease
	10.	Capital	Capital	Decrease
		Cash	Asset	Decrease

4.5

| | ASSETS | | | = LIABILITIES + CAPITAL | |
TRANS NO.	CASH	SUPPLIES	EQUIPMENT	ACCOUNTS PAYABLE	CAPITAL
1.	+9,600				+9,600
2.	−2,400		+2,400		
Balance	7,200		2,400		9,600
3.	−900				−900
Balance	6,300		2,400		8,700
4.			+6,600	+6,600	
Balance	6,300		9,000	6,600	8,700
5.	+1,500				+1,500
Balance	7,800		9,000	6,600	10,200
6.	+2,700				+2,700
Balance	10,500		9,000	6,600	12,900
7.	−480	+480			
Balance	10,020	480	9,000	6,600	12,900
8.	−1,200				−1,200
Balance	8,820	480	9,000	6,600	11,700
9.	−6,600			−6,600	
Balance	2,220	480	9,000		11,700
10.	−1,100				−1,100
Balance	1,120	480	9,000		10,600

BALANCE PROOF: Total of Assets: ___$10,600___ = Liabilities + Capital: ___$10,600___

	Accounts Affected	Account Classification	Change in Balance
	Either order:		
4.6 1.	Capital	Capital	Decrease
	Cash	Asset	Decrease
2.	Cash	Asset	Increase
	Capital	Capital	Increase
3.	Cash	Asset	Increase
	Capital	Capital	Increase
4.	Cash	Asset	Decrease
	Capital	Capital	Decrease
5.	Cash	Asset	Decrease
	Accts. Payable	Liability	Decrease
6.	Cash	Asset	Increase
	Capital	Capital	Increase
7.	Cash	Asset	Decrease
	Capital	Capital	Decrease
8.	Cash	Asset	Decrease
	Prepaid Ins.	Asset	Increase
9.	Cash	Asset	Decrease
	Supplies	Asset	Increase
10.	Cash	Asset	Increase
	Capital	Capital	Increase

	Accounts Affected	Account Classification	Change in Balance
11.	Cash	Asset	Decrease
	Capital	Capital	Decrease
12.	Cash	Asset	Decrease
	Capital	Capital	Decrease
13.	Cash	Asset	Decrease
	Accts. Payable	Liability	Decrease
14.	Cash	Asset	Increase
	Capital	Capital	Increase
15.	Cash	Asset	Decrease
	Capital	Capital	Decrease
16.	Cash	Asset	Increase
	Capital	Capital	Increase

	ASSETS			= LIABILITIES + CAPITAL	
TRANS NO.	*Cash*	*Supplies*	*Prepaid Insurance*	*Accounts Payable*	*J. King, Capital*
1.	*1,500*	*1,800*	*300*	*850*	*2,750*
2.	*–700*				*–700*
Balance	*800*	*1,800*	*300*	*850*	*2,050*
3.	*+600*				*+600*
Balance	*1,400*	*1,800*	*300*	*850*	*2,650*
4.	*+2,000*				*+2,000*
Balance	*3,400*	*1,800*	*300*	*850*	*4,650*
5.	*–25*				*–25*
Balance	*3,375*	*1,800*	*300*	*850*	*4,625*
6.	*–150*			*–150*	
Balance	*3,225*	*1,800*	*300*	*700*	*4,625*
7.	*+800*				*+800*
Balance	*4,025*	*1,800*	*300*	*700*	*5,425*
8.	*–45*				*–45*
Balance	*3,980*	*1,800*	*300*	*700*	*5,380*
9.	*–200*		*+200*		
Balance	*3,780*	*1,800*	*500*	*700*	*5,380*
10.	*–100*	*+100*			
Balance	*3,680*	*1,900*	*500*	*700*	*5,380*
11.	*+500*				*+500*
Balance	*4,180*	*1,900*	*500*	*700*	*5,880*
12.	*–200*				*–200*
Balance	*3,980*	*1,900*	*500*	*700*	*5,680*
13.	*–100*				*–100*
Balance	*3,880*	*1,900*	*500*	*700*	*5,580*
14.	*–350*			*–350*	
Balance	*3,530*	*1,900*	*500*	*350*	*5,580*
15.	*+700*				*+700*
Balance	*4,230*	*1,900*	*500*	*350*	*6,280*
16.	*–25*				*–25*
Balance	*4,205*	*1,900*	*500*	*350*	*6,255*
17.	*+150*				*+150*
Balance	*4,355*	*1,900*	*500*	*350*	*6,405*

4.7

BALANCE PROOF: Total of Assets: ___*$6,755*___ = Liabilities + Capital: ___*$6,755*___

	ASSETS				= LIABILITIES + CAPITAL	
TRANS NO.	Cash	Supplies	Prepaid Insurance	Equipment	Accounts Payable	H. Harrison, Capital
1.	2,500	1,150	1,800	2,400	1,850	6,000
2.	−900					−900
Balance	1,600	1,150	1,800	2,400	1,850	5,100
3.	+950					+950
Balance	2,550	1,150	1,800	2,400	1,850	6,050
4.	+1,800					+1,800
Balance	4,350	1,150	1,800	2,400	1,850	7,850
5.	−25					−25
Balance	4,325	1,150	1,800	2,400	1,850	7,825
6.	−1,150				−1,150	
Balance	3,175	1,150	1,800	2,400	700	7,825
7.	+800					+800
Balance	3,975	1,150	1,800	2,400	700	8,625
8.	−65					−65
Balance	3,910	1,150	1,800	2,400	700	8,560
9.	−800		+800			
Balance	3,110	1,150	2,600	2,400	700	8,560
10.	−600	+600				
Balance	2,510	1,750	2,600	2,400	700	8,560
11.	+750					+750
Balance	3,260	1,750	2,600	2,400	700	9,310
12.	−1,200					−1,200
Balance	2,060	1,750	2,600	2,400	700	8,110
13.	−400					−400
Balance	1,660	1,750	2,600	2,400	700	7,710
14.		+850			+850	
Balance	1,660	2,600	2,600	2,400	1,550	7,710
15.	+700					+700
Balance	2,360	2,600	2,600	2,400	1,550	8,410
16.	−225					−225
Balance	2,135	2,600	2,600	2,400	1,550	8,185
17.	+250					+250
Balance	2,385	2,600	2,600	2,400	1,550	8,435

4.8

BALANCE PROOF: Total of Assets: _____ $9,985_____ = Liabilities + Capital: _____$9,985_____

TRANS NO.	ASSETS					= LIABILITIES + CAPITAL		
	Cash	Accounts Rec.	Office Supplies	Equipment	Building	Accts. Payable	Notes Payable	J. Oats, Capital
1.	+50,000							+50,000
2.	–45,000				+150,000		+105,000	
Balance	5,000				150,000		105,000	50,000
3.				+500				+500
Balance	5,000			500	150,000		105,000	50,500
4.	–550		+550					
Balance	4,450		550	500	150,000		105,000	50,500
5.				+7,500		+7,500		
Balance	4,450		550	8,000	150,000	7,500	105,000	50,500
6.	+630							+630
Balance	5,080		550	8,000	150,000	7,500	105,000	51,130
7.	–250							–250
Balance	4,830		550	8,000	150,000	7,500	105,000	50,880
8.		+1,900						+1,900
Balance	4,830	1,900	550	8,000	150,000	7,500	105,000	52,780
9.	–750					–750		
Balance	4,080	1,900	550	8,000	150,000	6,750	105,000	52,780
10.	+1,900	–1,900						
Balance	5,980		550	8,000	150,000	6,750	105,000	52,780
11.	–650							–650
Balance	5,330		550	8,000	150,000	6,750	105,000	52,130
12.	–450							–450
Balance	4,880		550	8,000	150,000	6,750	105,000	51,680
13.	–2,000						–2,000	
Balance	2,880		550	8,000	150,000	6,750	103,000	51,680

4.9

BALANCE PROOF: Total of Assets: __$161,430__ = Liabilities + Capital: __$161,430__

Source Document – a document that provides the necessary information to make a journal entry.

Transaction – an action that changes the value of the assets, liabilities and capital of a business entity.

SECTION I

1.1	e	1.6	i
1.2	a	1.7	g
1.3	h	1.8	c
1.4	d	1.9	b
1.5	j	1.10	f

1.11

The Beauty Chateau Chart of Accounts			
a. *Assets*		f. *Liabilities*	
b. *Cash*	110	g. *Accounts Payable*	210
c. *Beauty Supplies*	120	h. *Notes Payable*	220
d. *Prepaid Insurance*	130	i. *Sales Tax Payable*	230
e. *Shop Equipment*	140		
		j. *Capital*	
		k. *Mary Murphy, Capital*	310
		l. *Mary Murphy, Drawing*	320

SECTION II

2.1

Harry's Hobby Shop					
Balance Sheet					
June 30, 20–					
Assets			Liabilities		
Cash	1550	00	Accounts Payable	1600	00
Supplies	1725	00			
Prepaid Insurance	675	00	Capital		
Equipment	4500	00	Harry Henderson, Capital	6850	00
Total Assets	8450	00	Total Liabilities & Capital	8450	00

2.2

Georgia's Flowers					
Balance Sheet					
July 31, 20–					
Assets			Liabilities		
Cash	1450	00	Accounts Payable 1600.00		
Supplies	725	00	Notes Payable 1200.00		
Prepaid Insurance	1600	00	Total Liabilities	2800	00
Equipment	5400	00			
			Capital		
			Georgia Jones, Capital	6375	00
Total Assets	9175	00	Total Liabilities & Capital	9175	00

SECTION III (see Self Test 3)

SECTION IV

4.1

ACCOUNT TITLE	ASSET	LIABILITY	OWNER'S EQUITY
a. Supplies	X		
b. Accounts Payable		X	
c. Cash	X		
d. Capital			X
e. Equipment	X		
f. Notes Payable		X	
g. Prepaid Insurance	X		
h. Sales Tax Payable		X	
i. Accounts Receivable	X		
j. Anything of value owned	X		
k. Any amount owed		X	
l. Professional library	X		
m. Withdrawals by owner			X
n. Automobile	X		
o. Owner's equity in anything owned			X

4.2

ACCOUNT TITLE	LEFT	RIGHT
a. Cash	X	
b. Notes Payable		X
c. Supplies	X	
d. Accounts Receivable	X	
e. Sales Tax Payable		X
f. Prepaid Insurance	X	
g. Accounts Payable		X
h. Capital		X

4.3

Item	Balance Sheet		Journal	
	Left	Right	Debit Column	Credit Column
a. Cash	*asset*		X	
b. Accounts Payable		*liability*		X
c. Supplies	*asset*		X	
d. Notes Payable		*liability*		X
e. Capital		*capital*		X
f. Prepaid Insurance	*asset*		X	

<table>
<tr><td colspan="4">Johnson's Service Station
Chart of Accounts</td></tr>
</table>

4.4

Assets		Liabilities	
Cash	*110*	*Accounts Payable*	*210*
Accounts Receivable	*120*	*Notes Payable*	*220*
Supplies	*130*	*Sales Tax Payable*	*230*
Prepaid Insurance	*140*		
Equipment	*150*	*Capital*	
		Mike Johnson, Capital	*310*

4.5   a. 4   g. 9

b. 10   h. 8

c. 3   i. 7

d. 5   j. 6

e. 1   k. 2

f. 11

4.6   a. 4   f. 9

b. 6   g. 5

c. 2   h. 7

d. 3   i. 8

e. 1

4.7

Green's Dentistry					
Balance Sheet					
January 1, 20–					
Assets			Liabilities		
Cash	1020	00	Accounts Payable	500	00
Supplies	480	00			
Equipment	9000	00	Capital		
			John Green, Capital	10000	00
Total Assets	10500	00	Total Liabilities & Capital	10500	00

4.8

Downs' Law Office					
Balance Sheet					
June 1, 20–					
Assets			Liabilities		
Cash	1400	00	Accounts Payable	1660	00
Law Library	2880	00			
Office Equipment	6880	00	Capital		
			Joanne Downs, Capital	9500	00
Total Assets	11160	00	Total Liabilities & Capital	11160	00

4.9

<table>
<tr><td colspan="6" align="center">*The Bicycle Shop*</td></tr>
<tr><td colspan="6" align="center">*Balance Sheet*</td></tr>
<tr><td colspan="6" align="center">*August 1, 20–*</td></tr>
<tr><td colspan="6"></td></tr>
<tr><td align="center">*Assets*</td><td></td><td></td><td align="center">*Liabilities*</td><td></td><td></td></tr>
<tr><td>*Cash*</td><td>1650</td><td>00</td><td>*Accounts Payable* 300.00</td><td></td><td></td></tr>
<tr><td>*Supplies*</td><td>750</td><td>00</td><td>*Notes Payable* 150.00</td><td></td><td></td></tr>
<tr><td>*Prepaid Insurance*</td><td>980</td><td>00</td><td>*Sales Tax Payable* 600.00</td><td></td><td></td></tr>
<tr><td>*Automobile*</td><td>6900</td><td>00</td><td>*Total Liabilities*</td><td>1050</td><td>00</td></tr>
<tr><td></td><td></td><td></td><td></td><td></td><td></td></tr>
<tr><td></td><td></td><td></td><td>*Capital*</td><td></td><td></td></tr>
<tr><td></td><td></td><td></td><td>*Harry Smith, Capital*</td><td>9230</td><td>00</td></tr>
<tr><td align="center">*Total Assets*</td><td>10280</td><td>00</td><td>*Total Liabilities & Capital*</td><td>10280</td><td>00</td></tr>
</table>

4.10 Journal for **Clean-Rite Company**:

JOURNAL						Page 1	
Date 20—	Account Title and Explanation	Doc No.	Post. Ref.	General Debit		General Credit	
Jan. 1	*Cash*		110	4105	00		
	Supplies		120	2000	00		
	Prepaid Insurance		130	500	00		
	Accounts Payable		210			350	00
	James King, Capital	M1	310			6255	00

4.11   Journal for **Map-It**:

JOURNAL								**Page** *1*	
Date 20—	**Account Title and Explanation**	**Doc No.**	**Post. Ref.**	**General Debit**		**General Credit**	
Sept. 1	*Cash*		110	2360	00		
	Supplies		120	2600	00		
	Prepaid Insurance		130	2600	00		
	Equipment		140	2400	00		
	Accounts Payable		210			1550	00
	Henry Harrison, Capital	M1	310			8410	00

4.12   Ledger accounts for **Clean-Rite Company** after opening entry from 4.10 is posted:

							Balance			
Account Title: *Cash*									**Account No.** *110*	
Date 20—	**Explanation**	**Post. Ref.**	**Debit**		**Credit**		**Debit**		**Credit**	
Jan. 1	*Opening entry*	*J1*	4105	00			4105	00		

							Balance			
Account Title: *Supplies*									**Account No.** *120*	
Date 20—	**Explanation**	**Post. Ref.**	**Debit**		**Credit**		**Debit**		**Credit**	
Jan. 1	*Opening entry*	*J1*	2000	00			2000	00		

							Balance			
Account Title: *Prepaid Insurance*									**Account No.** *130*	
Date 20—	**Explanation**	**Post. Ref.**	**Debit**		**Credit**		**Debit**		**Credit**	
Jan. 1	*Opening entry*	*J1*	500	00			500	00		

4.12   (cont'd)

Account Title: *Accounts Payable*							Account No. *210*			
Date 20—		Explanation	Post. Ref.	Debit		Credit		Balance		
								Debit	Credit	
Jan.	1	Opening entry	J1			350	00		350	00

Account Title: *James King, Capital*							Account No. *310*			
Date 20—		Explanation	Post. Ref.	Debit		Credit		Balance		
								Debit	Credit	
Jan.	1	Opening entry	J1			6255	00		6255	00

4.13   Ledger accounts for **Map-It** after opening entry from 4.11 is posted:

Account Title: *Cash*							Account No. *110*			
Date 20—		Explanation	Post. Ref.	Debit		Credit		Balance		
								Debit	Credit	
Sept.	1	Opening entry	J1	2360	00			2360	00	

Account Title: *Supplies*							Account No. *120*			
Date 20—		Explanation	Post. Ref.	Debit		Credit		Balance		
								Debit	Credit	
Sept.	1	Opening entry	J1	2600	00			2600	00	

4.13   (cont'd)

Account Title: *Prepaid Insurance*   **Account No.** *130*

Date 20—		Explanation	Post. Ref.	Debit		Credit		Balance Debit		Balance Credit	
Sept.	1	Opening entry	J1	2600	00			2600	00		

Account Title: *Equipment*   **Account No.** *140*

Date 20—		Explanation	Post. Ref.	Debit		Credit		Balance Debit		Balance Credit	
Sept.	1	Opening entry	J1	2400	00			2400	00		

Account Title: *Accounts Payable*   **Account No.** *210*

Date 20—		Explanation	Post. Ref.	Debit		Credit		Balance Debit		Balance Credit	
Sept.	1	Opening entry	J1			1550	00			1550	00

Account Title: *James King, Capital*   **Account No.** *310*

Date 20—		Explanation	Post. Ref.	Debit		Credit		Balance Debit		Balance Credit	
Sept.	1	Opening entry	J1			8410	00			8410	00

4.14

Al's TV Service Chart of Accounts			
Assets		**Liabilities**	
Cash	110	Accounts Payable	210
Accounts Receivable	120	Notes Payable	220
Office Supplies	130	Sales Tax Payable	230
TV Supplies	140		
Equipment	150	**Capital**	
		Al Stevenson, Capital	310

4.15

Al's TV Service					
Balance Sheet					
March 1, 20–					
Assets			**Liabilities**		
Cash	1850	00	Accounts Payable 450.00		
Accounts Receivable	690	00	Notes Payable 1230.00		
Office Supplies	980	00	Sales Tax Payable 750.00		
TV Supplies	1150	00	Total Liabilities	2430	00
Equipment	5640	00			
			Capital		
			Al Stevenson, Capital	7880	00
Total Assets	10310	00	Total Liabilities & Capital	10310	00

4.16

	JOURNAL							Page *1*	
Date 20—	Account Title and Explanation	Doc No.	Post. Ref.	General Debit		General Credit			
Mar. 1	Cash		110	1850	00				
	Accounts Receivable		120	690	00				
	Office Supplies		130	980	00				
	TV Supplies		140	1150	00				
	Equipment		150	5640	00				
	Accounts Payable		210			450	00		
	Notes Payable		220			1230	00		
	Sales Tax Payable		230			750	00		
	Al Stevenson, Capital	M1	310			7880	00		

4.17

Account Title: *Cash*								Account No. *110*		
Date 20—	Explanation	Post. Ref.	Debit		Credit		Balance			
							Debit		Credit	
Mar. 1	Opening entry	J1	1850	00			1850	00		

Account Title: *Accounts Receivable*								Account No. *120*		
Date 20—	Explanation	Post. Ref.	Debit		Credit		Balance			
							Debit		Credit	
Mar. 1	Opening entry	J1	690	00			690	00		

Account Title: *Office Supplies*								Account No. *130*		
Date 20—	Explanation	Post. Ref.	Debit		Credit		Balance			
							Debit		Credit	
Mar. 1	Opening entry	J1	980	00			980	00		

4.17 (cont'd)

Account Title: *TV Supplies*   **Account No.** *140*

Date 20—		Explanation	Post. Ref.	Debit		Credit		Balance			
								Debit		Credit	
Mar.	1	Opening entry	J1	1150	00			1150	00		

Account Title: *Equipment*   **Account No.** *150*

Date 20—		Explanation	Post. Ref.	Debit		Credit		Balance			
								Debit		Credit	
Mar.	1	Opening entry	J1	5640	00			5640	00		

Account Title: *Accounts Payable*   **Account No.** *210*

Date 20—		Explanation	Post. Ref.	Debit		Credit		Balance			
								Debit		Credit	
Mar.	1	Opening entry	J1			450	00			450	00

Account Title: *Notes Payable*   **Account No.** *220*

Date 20—		Explanation	Post. Ref.	Debit		Credit		Balance			
								Debit		Credit	
Mar.	1	Opening entry	J1			1230	00			1230	00

Account Title: *Sales Tax Payable*   **Account No.** *230*

Date 20—		Explanation	Post. Ref.	Debit		Credit		Balance			
								Debit		Credit	
Mar.	1	Opening entry	J1			750	00			750	00

4.17 (cont'd)

Account Title: *Al Stevenson, Capital*						Account No. *310*		
Date 20—	Explanation	Post. Ref.	Debit		Credit		Balance Debit	Balance Credit
Mar. 1	Opening entry	J1			7880 00			7880 00

4.18

Barry Holt, Consultant Chart of Accounts			
Assets		**Liabilities**	
Cash	110	Accounts Payable	210
Accounts Receivable	120	Mortgage Payable	220
Office Supplies	130	Notes Payable	230
Prepaid Insurance	140		
Land	150	**Capital**	
Building	160	Barry Holt, Capital	310

4.19

Barry Holt, Consultant					
Balance Sheet					
October 1, 20–					
Assets			**Liabilities**		
Cash	5600	00	Accounts Payable 1400.00		
Accounts Receivable	8800	00	Mortgage Payable 21700.00		
Office Supplies	500	00	Notes Payable 25000.00		
Prepaid Insurance	1200	00	Total Liabilities	48100	00
Land	18000	00			
Building	47000	00	**Capital**		
			Barry Holt, Capital	33000	00
Total Assets	81100	00	Total Liabilities & Capital	81100	00

4.20

		JOURNAL						Page *1*	
Date 20—		Account Title and Explanation	Doc No.	Post. Ref.	General Debit			General Credit	
Oct.	1	Cash		110	5600	00			
		Accounts Receivable		120	8800	00			
		Office Supplies		130	500	00			
		Prepaid Insurance		140	1200	00			
		Land		150	18000	00			
		Building		160	47000	00			
		Accounts Payable		210				1400	00
		Mortgage Payable		220				21700	00
		Notes Payable		230				25000	00
		Barry Holt, Capital	M1	310				33000	00

4.21

Account Title: *Cash*								Account No. *110*		
Date 20—		Explanation	Post. Ref.	Debit		Credit		Balance		
								Debit		Credit
Oct.	1	Opening entry	J1	5600	00			5600	00	

Account Title: *Accounts Receivable*								Account No. *120*		
Date 20—		Explanation	Post. Ref.	Debit		Credit		Balance		
								Debit		Credit
Oct.	1	Opening entry	J1	8800	00			8800	00	

Account Title: *Office Supplies*								Account No. *130*		
Date 20—		Explanation	Post. Ref.	Debit		Credit		Balance		
								Debit		Credit
Oct.	1	Opening entry	J1	500	00			500	00	

4.21 (cont'd)

Account Title: *Prepaid Insurance*							Account No. *140*	
Date 20—		Explanation	Post. Ref.	Debit		Credit	Balance Debit	Balance Credit
Oct.	1	Opening entry	J1	1200	00		1200 00	

Account Title: *Land*							Account No. *150*	
Date 20—		Explanation	Post. Ref.	Debit		Credit	Balance Debit	Balance Credit
Oct.	1	Opening entry	J1	18000	00		18000 00	

Account Title: *Building*							Account No. *160*	
Date 20—		Explanation	Post. Ref.	Debit		Credit	Balance Debit	Balance Credit
Oct.	1	Opening entry	J1	47000	00		47000 00	

Account Title: *Accounts Payable*							Account No. *210*	
Date 20—		Explanation	Post. Ref.	Debit	Credit		Balance Debit	Balance Credit
Oct.	1	Opening entry	J1		1400	00		1400 00

Account Title: *Mortgage Payable*							Account No. *220*	
Date 20—		Explanation	Post. Ref.	Debit	Credit		Balance Debit	Balance Credit
Oct.	1	Opening entry	J1		21700	00		21700 00

4.21 (cont'd)

Account Title: *Notes Payable*								Account No. *230*			
Date 20—		Explanation	Post. Ref.	Debit		Credit		Balance			
								Debit		Credit	
Oct.	1	*Opening entry*	*J1*			25000	00			25000	00

Account Title: *Barry Holt, Capital*								Account No. *310*			
Date 20—		Explanation	Post. Ref.	Debit		Credit		Balance			
								Debit		Credit	
Oct.	1	*Opening entry*	*J1*			33000	00			33000	00

4.22

ACCOUNT		CLASSIFICATION
a.	Cash	*Asset*
b.	Mortgage Payable	*Liability*
c.	Office Supplies	*Asset*
d.	Anything of value owned	*Asset*
e.	Accounts Payable	*Liability*
f.	Owner's equity	*Capital*
g.	Prepaid Insurance	*Asset*
h.	Any amount owed	*Liability*
i.	Accounts Receivable	*Asset*

4.23

	Jones' Trucking					
	Balance Sheet					
	January 1, 20–					
Assets			*Liabilities*		
Cash	2500	00	*Accounts Payable*	1850	00
Supplies	1150	00			
Prepaid Insurance	1800	00	*Capital*		
Equipment	2400	00	*George Jones, Capital*	6000	00
Total Assets	7850	00	*Total Liabilities & Capital*	7850	00

4.24

		JOURNAL					Page 1	
Date 20—		Account Title and Explanation	Doc No.	Post. Ref.	General Debit		General Credit	
Jan.	1	*Cash*			2500	00		
		Supplies			1150	00		
		Prepaid Insurance			1800	00		
		Equipment			2400	00		
		Accounts Payable					1850	00
		George Jones, Capital	M1				6000	00

OPTIONAL EXERCISES FOR EXTRA CREDIT

1. journalizing and posting

2. it provides evidence that a transaction has occurred

3. a business form used to sort and summarize changes in a specific balance sheet item

4. it provides a list of all the accounts used by a business, and it provides a classification and numbering system for those accounts

5. to show the relationship between assets and the claims against those assets

6. the accounting equation must always remain in balance. The total of the items on the left side (assets) must equal the total of the items on the right side (liabilities & capital)

7. Assets, Liabilities & Capital

8. at least two

9. the general journal

10. 1. Write the account title in the correct space on the ledger account.
    2. Write the account number in the correct space on the ledger account.

11. it provides a cross-reference to trace an entry from the journal to the ledger account

12. the debit is written first

13.

Stone's Designs Chart of Accounts			
Assets		**Liabilities**	
Cash	110	**Accounts Payable**	210
Office Supplies	120		
Prepaid Insurance	130	*Capital*	
Equipment	140	*Jane Stone, Capital*	310

14.

Stone's Designs					
Balance Sheet					
September 1, 20–					
Assets			Liabilities		
Cash	1575	00	Accounts Payable	9590	00
Office Supplies	675	00			
Prepaid Insurance	1125	00	Capital		
Equipment	12675	00	Jane Stone, Capital	6460	00
Total Assets	16050	00	Total Liabilities & Capital	16050	00

15.

JOURNAL						Page 1			
Date 20—		Account Title and Explanation	Doc No.	Post. Ref.	General Debit		General Credit		
Sept.	1	Cash		110	1575	00			
		Office Supplies		120	675	00			
		Prepaid Insurance		130	1125	00			
		Equipment		140	12675	00			
		Accounts Payable		210			9590	00	
		Jane Stone, Capital	M1	310			6460	00	

16.–17.

| Account Title: *Cash* | | | | | Account No. *110* | | | | |

Date 20—		Explanation	Post. Ref.	Debit		Credit		Balance			
								Debit		Credit	
Sept.	1	Opening entry	J1	1575	00			1575	00		

| Account Title: *Office Supplies* | | | | | Account No. *120* | | | | |

Date 20—		Explanation	Post. Ref.	Debit		Credit		Balance			
								Debit		Credit	
Sept.	1	Opening entry	J1	675	00			675	00		

| Account Title: *Prepaid Insurance* | | | | | Account No. *130* | | | | |

Date 20—		Explanation	Post. Ref.	Debit		Credit		Balance			
								Debit		Credit	
Sept.	1	Opening entry	J1	1125	00			1125	00		

| Account Title: *Equipment* | | | | | Account No. *140* | | | | |

Date 20—		Explanation	Post. Ref.	Debit		Credit		Balance			
								Debit		Credit	
Sept.	1	Opening entry	J1	12675	00			12675	00		

16.–17.   (cont'd)

Account Title: *Accounts Payable*								Account No. *210*		
Date 20—		Explanation	Post. Ref.	Debit		Credit		Balance		
								Debit	Credit	
Sept.	1	Opening entry	J1			9590	00		9590	00

Account Title: *Jane Stone, Capital*								Account No. *310*		
Date 20—		Explanation	Post. Ref.	Debit		Credit		Balance		
								Debit	Credit	
Sept.	1	Opening entry	J1			6460	00		6460	00

VOCABULARY

Account – a record that summarizes all the characteristics of a single item of the equation.

Account Balance – the computed balance of an account after all debits and credits have been posted.

Account Title – the name given to any account.

Accounting Equation – a mathematical equation that illustrates the relationship between assets, liabilities and owner's equity (capital): Assets = Liabilities + Capital.

Asset – anything of value owned by a business.

Balance Sheet – a form that shows the financial position of a business on a specific date.

Chart of Accounts – a list of all accounts used by an entity indicating the identifying number, the account title and classification of each accounting equation item.

Chronological – in order by date.

Compound Entry – a journal entry that contains more than two accounts.

Contra Account – an account that has a negative effect on a controlling account.

Credit – refers to any entry made in the right-hand amount column.

Debit – refers to any entry made in the left-hand amount column.

Double-entry Accounting – each financial transaction has a double effect and is recorded so that the total of the debit amounts is always equal to the total of the credit amounts.

Entry – a transaction recorded in journal.

Expenses – the cost of goods and services used in the operation of a business.

General Ledger – contains all the accounts needed to prepare financial statements.

Income – the difference between revenue from the sale of goods and services and the expenses that come from operating the business and making the sales.

Income Statement – a financial statement that reports the revenue, expenses and net income or net loss of a business for a specific period of time.

Journal – a business form used for recording accounting information in chronological order with transactions analyzed in terms of the accounts to be debited and credited.

Journalizing – recording information in chronological order in the journal, using the source document as evidence of the business transaction.

Ledger – a group of accounts.

Opening an Account – writing the account name and number as the heading for the account.

Permanent Accounts – balance sheet accounts (assets, liabilities & capital) that provide data from one accounting period to the next.

Posting – the process of transferring the information from a journal entry to the ledger account.

Revenue – the increase in owner's equity caused by the inflow of assets from the sale of goods and services.

Source Document – a written or printed paper that provides evidence that a transaction occurred and gives the information needed to analyze the transaction; e.g., a purchase invoice, a check stub, a receipt, a memorandum, etc.

T Account – an accounting device used to analyze business transactions.

Temporary Accounts – accounts (such as Revenue and Expenses) that gather data for one accounting period only; accounts used to compute net income for each accounting period.

Transaction – changes the value of the assets, liabilities and capital of a business entity.

SECTION I

1.1

Cash	
a. *Debit*	*Credit*
b. *Balance*	
c. *Increase*	*Decrease*

1.2

Supplies	
a. *Debit*	*Credit*
b. *Balance*	
c. *Increase*	*Decrease*

1.3

Prepaid Insurance	
a. *Debit*	*Credit*
b. *Balance*	
c. *Increase*	*Decrease*

1.4

Accts. Pay./Fox Film Co.	
a. *Debit*	*Credit*
b.	*Balance*
c. *Decrease*	*Increase*

1.5

Accts. Pay./MGM Film Co.	
a. *Debit*	*Credit*
b.	*Balance*
c. *Decrease*	*Increase*

1.6

Accts. Pay./Mortgage Payable	
a. *Debit*	*Credit*
b.	*Balance*
c. *Decrease*	*Increase*

1.7

James Smith, Capital	
a. *Debit*	*Credit*
b.	*Balance*
c. *Decrease*	*Increase*

1.8

James Smith, Drawing	
a. *Debit*	*Credit*
b. *Balance*	
c. *Increase*	*Decrease*

1.9

Video Sales & Rental	
a. *Debit*	*Credit*
b.	*Balance*
c. *Decrease*	*Increase*

1.10

Advertising Expense	
a. *Debit*	*Credit*
b. *Balance*	
c. *Increase*	*Decrease*

1.11

Miscellaneous Expense	
a. *Debit*	*Credit*
b. *Balance*	
c. *Increase*	*Decrease*

1.12

Utilities Expense	
a. *Debit*	*Credit*
b. *Balance*	
c. *Increase*	*Decrease*

1.13

Trans Date	Accounts Affected	Account Classification	Normal Account Balance		Changes in Account Balance		How Change is Entered	
			Debit	Credit	Increase	Decrease	Debit	Credit
5-1	Cash	Asset	✔		✔		✔	
	K. Bates, Capital	Capital		✔	✔			✔
5-2	Prepaid Ins.	Asset	✔		✔		✔	
	Cash	Asset	✔			✔		✔
5-3	Supplies	Asset	✔		✔		✔	
	Cash	Asset	✔			✔		✔
5-6	Supplies	Asset	✔		✔		✔	
	Accts. Payable	Liability		✔	✔			✔
5-7	Cash	Asset	✔		✔		✔	
	Sales	Revenue		✔	✔			✔
5-8	Utilities Exp.	Expense	✔		✔		✔	
	Cash	Asset	✔			✔		✔
5-9	Advertising Exp.	Expense	✔		✔		✔	
	Cash	Asset	✔			✔		✔
5-10	Accts. Payable	Liability		✔		✔	✔	
	Cash	Asset	✔			✔		✔
5-11	Cash	Asset	✔		✔		✔	
	Sales	Revenue		✔	✔			✔
5-12	Misc. Exp.	Expense	✔		✔		✔	
	Cash	Asset	✔			✔		✔
5-13	K. Bates, Dwg.	[Contra] Capital	✔		✔		✔	
	Cash	Asset	✔			✔		✔
5-14	Rent Exp.	Expense	✔		✔		✔	
	Cash	Asset	✔			✔		✔

1.14–1.15

Cash			
(5-1)	6500.00	*(5-2)*	450.00
(5-7)	890.00	*(5-3)*	75.00
(5-11)	625.00	*(5-8)*	125.00
		(5-9)	50.00
		(5-10)	35.00
		(5-12)	6.75
		(5-13)	150.00
		(5-14)	350.00

Supplies	
(5-3)	75.00
(5-6)	100.00

Prepaid Insurance	
(5-2)	450.00

Accounts Payable			
(5-10)	35.00	*(5-6)*	100.00

Kathy Bates, Capital			
		(5-1)	6500.00

Kathy Bates, Drawing	
(5-13)	150.00

Sales			
		(5-7)	890.00
		(5-11)	625.00

Advertising Expense	
(5-10)	50.00

Miscellaneous Expense	
(5-12)	6.75

Rent Expense	
(5-14)	350.00

Utilities Expense	
(5-8)	125.00

1.16

Trans Date	Accounts Affected	Account Classification	Normal Account Balance		Changes in Account Balance		How Change is Entered	
			Debit	Credit	Increase	Decrease	Debit	Credit
3-1	Cash	Asset	✔		✔		✔	
	G. Hand, Capital	Capital		✔	✔			✔
3-2	Supplies	Asset	✔		✔		✔	
	Visa	Liability		✔	✔			✔
3-3	Rent Exp.	Expense	✔		✔		✔	
	Cash	Asset	✔			✔		✔
3-4	Cash	Asset	✔		✔		✔	
	Sales	Revenue		✔	✔			✔
3-5	Visa	Liability		✔		✔	✔	
	Cash	Asset	✔			✔		✔
3-6	Trans. Fee. Exp.	Expense	✔		✔		✔	
	Cash	Asset	✔			✔		✔
3-7	Cash	Asset	✔		✔		✔	
	Sales	Revenue		✔	✔			✔
3-8	Supplies	Asset	✔		✔		✔	
	Cash	Asset	✔			✔		✔
3-9	Prepaid Ins.	Asset	✔		✔		✔	
	Cash	Asset	✔			✔		✔
3-10	Supplies	Asset	✔		✔		✔	
	MasterCard	Liability		✔	✔			✔
3-11	Supplies	Asset	✔		✔		✔	
	Cash	Asset	✔			✔		✔
3-12	Cash	Asset	✔		✔		✔	
	Sales	Revenue		✔	✔			✔
3-13	Utilities Exp.	Expense	✔		✔		✔	
	Cash	Asset	✔			✔		✔
3-14	Advertising Exp.	Expense	✔		✔		✔	
	Cash	Asset	✔			✔		✔
3-15	Misc. Exp.	Expense	✔		✔		✔	
	Cash	Asset	✔			✔		✔
3-16	Cash	Asset	✔		✔		✔	
	Sales	Revenue		✔	✔			✔
3-17	G. Hand, Dwg. [Contra] Capital		✔		✔		✔	
	Cash	Asset	✔			✔		✔
3-18	Cash	Asset	✔		✔		✔	
	Sales	Revenue		✔	✔			✔

1.17–1.18

Cash			
(3-1)	2000.00	(3-3)	500.00
(3-4)	650.00	(3-5)	250.00
(3-7)	500.00	(3-6)	90.00
(3-12)	950.00	(3-8)	400.00
(3-16)	900.00	(3-9)	350.00
(3-18)	900.00	(3-11)	600.00
		(3-13)	95.00
		(3-14)	230.00
		(3-15)	25.00
		(3-17)	800.00

Supplies	
(3-2)	500.00
(3-8)	400.00
(3-10)	60.00
(3-11)	600.00

Prepaid Insurance	
(3-9)	350.00

Visa Credit Card			
(3-5)	250.00	(3-2)	500.00

MasterCard Credit Card			
		(3-10)	60.00

George Hand, Capital			
		(3-1)	2000.00

George Hand, Drawing	
(3-17)	800.00

Sales			
		(3-4)	650.00
		(3-7)	500.00
		(3-12)	950.00
		(3-16)	520.00
		(3-18)	900.00

Advertising Expense	
(3-14)	230.00

Miscellaneous Expense	
(3-15)	25.00

Rent Expense	
(3-3)	500.00

Transfer Fee Expense	
(3-6)	90.00

Utilities Expense	
(3-13)	95.00

1.19–1.20

Cash			
(6-1)	52000.00	(6-2)	45000.00
(6-7)	8500.00	(6-3)	3000.00
(6-12)	210.00	(6-5)	720.00
		(6-6)	600.00
		(6-8)	150.00
		(6-9)	60.00
		(6-11)	600.00
		(6-13)	1500.00

Notes Payable			
		(6-2)	60000.00

Kay Black, Capital			
		(6-1)	60000.00

Accounts Receivable			
(6-10)	210.00	(6-12)	210.00

Kay Black, Drawing			
(6-13)	1500.00		

Office Supplies			
(6-4)	60.00		

Appraisal Fees			
		(6-10)	210.00

Office Equipment			
(6-1)	8000.00		
(6-5)	720.00		

Commissions			
		(6-7)	8500.00

Office Building			
(6-2)	105000.00		

Advertising Expense			
(6-3)	3000.00		
(6-8)	150.00		

Accounts Payable			
(6-9)	60.00	(6-4)	60.00

Office Salaries Expense			
(6-6)	600.00		
(6-11)	600.00		

SECTION II

2.1

JOURNAL									Page 1	
Date 20—		Account Title and Explanation	Doc No.	Post. Ref.	General Debit			General Credit		
May	1	Cash			14000	00				
		Josh Smith, Capital	R1					14000	00	
	3	Prepaid Insurance			1300	00				
		Cash	Ck1					1300	00	
	5	Supplies			1400	00				
		Jones Supply Co.	P1					1400	00	
	5	Rent Expense			750	00				
		Cash	Ck2					750	00	
	7	Miscellaneous Expense			5	00				
		Cash	Ck3					5	00	
	8	Supplies			1050	00				
		Cash	Ck4					1050	00	
	8	Cash			650	00				
		Sales	T8					650	00	
	9	Jones Supply Co.			1400	00				
		Cash	Ck5					1400	00	
	10	Repair Expense			85	00				
		Cash	Ck6					85	00	
	11	Advertising Expense			110	00				
		Cash	Ck7					110	00	
	12	Cash			1150	00				
		Sales	T12					1150	00	
	14	Utilities Expense			75	00				
		Cash	Ck8					75	00	
	14	Cash			550	00				
		Sales	T14					550	00	
	15	Josh Smith, Drawing			450	00				
		Cash	Ck9					450	00	
	16	Cash			675	00				
		Sales	T16					675	00	

2.2

		JOURNAL						**Page** *1*	
Date 20—		**Account Title and Explanation**	**Doc No.**	**Post. Ref.**	**General Debit**		**General Credit**		
June	1	*Cash*			13000	00			
		Donna Jenkins, Capital	R1				13000	00	
	2	*Rent Expense*			950	00			
		Cash	Ck1				950	00	
	3	*Supplies*			3000	00			
		Office Max	P1				3000	00	
	3	*Prepaid Insurance*			3500	00			
		Cash	Ck2				3500	00	
	6	*Cash*			1500	00			
		Search Fees	T6				1500	00	
	7	*Supplies*			650	00			
		Cash	Ck3				650	00	
	8	*Office Max*			1500	00			
		Cash	Ck4				1500	00	
	9	*Repair Expense*			75	00			
		Cash	Ck5				75	00	
	10	*Utilities Expense*			110	00			
		Cash	Ck6				110	00	
	12	*Cash*			950	00			
		Search Fees	T12				950	00	
	13	*Miscellaneous Expense*			35	00			
		Cash	Ck7				35	00	
	15	*Donna Jenkins, Drawing*			550	00			
		Cash	Ck8				550	00	
	16	*Office Equipment*			975	00			
		Cash	Ck9				975	00	
	17	*Cash*			1800	00			
		Search Fees	T17				1800	00	
	19	*Office Equipment*			3800	00			
		Wilson Supply House	P2				3800	00	

2.3

	Date 20—		Account Title and Explanation	Doc No.	Post. Ref.	General Debit		General Credit	
JOURNAL								Page *1*	
June	1		*Cash*			20000	00		
			Dustin Harrison, Capital	*R1*				20000	00
	2		*Rent Expense*			900	00		
			Cash	*Ck1*				900	00
	3		*Supplies*			1600	00		
			Cash	*Ck2*				1600	00
	4		*Equipment*			18000	00		
			Day's Equipment Supply Co.	*P1*				18000	00
	5		*Prepaid Insurance*			600	00		
			Cash	*Ck3*				600	00
	5		*Cash*			1900	00		
			Service Sales	*T5*				1900	00
	8		*Day's Equipment Supply Co.*			1200	00		
			Cash	*Ck4*				1200	00
	9		*Repair Expense*			65	00		
			Cash	*Ck5*				65	00
	9		*Salary Expense*			789	00		
			Cash	*Ck6*				789	00
	10		*Supplies*			1300	00		
			Ceria Supply Co.	*P2*				1300	00
	10		*Advertising Expense*			75	00		
			Cash	*Ck7*				75	00
	11		*Dustin Harrison, Drawing*			450	00		
			Cash	*Ck8*				450	00

2.4

		JOURNAL						Page 2	
Date 20—		Account Title and Explanation	Doc No.	Post. Ref.	General Debit		General Credit		
June	12	Supplies			980	00		
		Cash	Ck9				980	00
	13	Cash			3450	00		
		Service Sales	T13				3450	00
	13	Supplies			800	00		
		Ceria Supply Co.	P3				800	00
	14	Salary Expense			989	00		
		Cash	Ck10				989	00
	15	Day's Equipment Supply Co.			1200	00		
		Cash	Ck11				1200	00
	16	Cash			3590	00		
		Service Sales	T16				3590	00
	19	Ceria Supply Co.			1300	00		
		Cash	Ck12				1300	00
	20	Prepaid Insurance			1210	00		
		Cash	Ck13				1210	00
	22	Advertising Expense			85	00		
		Cash	Ck14				85	00
	23	Dustin Harrison, Drawing			550	00		
		Cash	Ck15				550	00
	30	Salary Expense			780	00		
		Cash	Ck16				780	00
	30	Utilities Expense			56	00		
		Cash	Ck17				56	00

SECTION III

3.1

Trans.	Accounts Affected	Account Classification	Normal Account Balance		Changes in Account Balance		How Change is Entered	
			Debit	Credit	Increase	Decrease	Debit	Credit
a.	Cash	Asset	✔		✔		✔	
	J. Ryan, Capital	Capital		✔	✔			✔
b.	Building	Asset	✔		✔		✔	
	Mortgage Pay.	Liability		✔	✔			✔
c.	Cash	Asset	✔		✔		✔	
	Sales	Revenue		✔	✔			✔
d.	Rent Expense	Expense	✔		✔		✔	
	Cash	Asset	✔			✔		✔
e.	Supplies	Asset	✔		✔		✔	
	Cash	Asset	✔			✔		✔
f.	J. Ryan, Dwg.	[Contra] Capital	✔		✔		✔	
	Cash	Asset	✔			✔		✔
g.	Supplies	Asset	✔		✔		✔	
	Accts. Pay.	Liability		✔	✔			✔
h.	Prepaid Ins.	Asset	✔		✔		✔	
	Cash	Asset	✔			✔		✔
i.	Cash	Asset	✔		✔		✔	
	Sales	Revenue		✔	✔			✔
j.	Repairs Exp.	Expense	✔		✔		✔	
	Cash	Asset	✔			✔		✔
k.	Advertising Exp.	Expense	✔		✔		✔	
	Cash	Asset	✔			✔		✔
l.	Accts. Pay.	Liability		✔		✔	✔	
	Cash	Asset	✔			✔		✔

3.2

JOURNAL								Page *1*	
Date 20—		Account Title and Explanation	Doc No.	Post. Ref.	General Debit			General Credit	
Apr.	1	Cash			38000	00			
		Office Equipment			10000	00			
		Carlson Black, Capital	R1					48000	00
	2	Land			32000	00			
		Building			100000	00			
		Notes Payable						99000	00
		Cash	Ck100					33000	00
	3	Office Supplies			75	00			
		Accounts Payable	P2					75	00
	4	Automobile			7500	00			
		Cash	Ck101					7500	00
	5	Salary Expense			600	00			
		Cash	Ck102					600	00
	6	Cash			8700	00			
		Commissions	R2					8700	00
	7	Advertising Expense			250	00			
		Cash	Ck103					250	00
	8	Accounts Payable			75	00			
		Cash	Ck104					75	00
	9	Office Equipment			1840	00			
		Accounts Payable	P3					1840	00
	10	Accounts Receivable			210	00			
		Appraisal Fees	M1					210	00
	11	Salary Expense			640	00			
		Cash	Ck105					640	00
	12	Cash			210	00			
		Accounts Receivable	R3					210	00
	13	Carlson Black, Drawing			1500	00			
		Cash	Ck106					1500	00

3.3

Cash			
A.	30000.00	B.	15000.00
D.	6000.00	C.	1500.00
		E.	600.00
		F.	1800.00
		G.	680.00

George Sims, Capital	
	A. 30000.00

Office Supplies	
E. 600.00	

Commissions	
	D. 6000.00

Prepaid Insurance	
F. 1800.00	

Rent Expense	
C. 1500.00	

Equipment	
B. 15000.00	

Travel Expense	
G. 680.00	

OPTIONAL EXERCISES FOR EXTRA CREDIT

JOURNAL						Page 4		
Date 20—		Account Title and Explanation	Doc No.	Post. Ref.	General Debit		General Credit	
Apr.	22	Cash			1900	00		
		Commissions	R1				1900	00
	23	Office Supplies			1000	00		
		Cash	Ck101				1000	00
	24	Cash			2500	00		
		Kay Clark, Capital	R2				2500	00
	25	Utilities Expense			640	00		
		Cash	Ck102				640	00
	26	Cash			6000	00		
		Notes Payable	M1				6000	00
	27	Kay Clark, Drawing			600	00		
		Cash	Ck103				600	00
	28	Cash			750	00		
		Commissions	R3				750	00
	30	Utilities Expense			78	00		
		Cash	Ck104				78	00

VOCABULARY

Account – a device use to summarize all the changes that affect a single item in the accounting equation.

Account Balance – the difference between the debits and credits recorded in an account.

Account Number – the number assigned to an account in the ledger.

Balance Column Account – an account that has debit and credit columns for entering changes in the account and a column for entering the new account balance after each debit or credit is posted to the account.

Balance Sheet – a form that shows the financial position of a business on a specific date.

Book of Original Entry – a journal in which transactions are first recorded.

Book of Secondary Entry – a ledger to which amounts from the journal are posted.

Chart of Accounts – a list of all the accounts used by a business entity.

File Maintenance – the procedure of arranging accounts in a general ledger, inserting and deleting accounts, and keeping records current.

General Ledger – a book that contains all of the accounts needed to prepare the financial reports of a business entity.

Income Statement – a financial statement that reports the revenue, expenses, and net income or net loss of a business for a specific period of time.

Ledger – a group of accounts.

Opening an Account – writing the account title and number on the heading line of an account.

Opening Entry – the first entry made in a general journal that opens the accounts in a new set of books.

Posting – transferring information from a journal entry to a ledger account.

Proving Cash – the process of determining whether the amount of cash, both on hand and in the bank, is the same amount that exists in the accounting records.

Trial Balance – a proof (test) to show that the total debit balances in the ledger equal the total credit balances.

SECTION I (see Self Test 1)

SECTION II

2.1

JOURNAL									Page /	

JOURNAL — Page /

Date 20—		Account Title and Explanation	Doc No.	Post. Ref.	General Debit		General Credit	
Jan.	1	Cash		110	15000	00		
		Art Kline, Capital	M1	310			15000	00
	2	Cash		110	1500	00		
		Sales	T12	410			1500	00
	5	Advertising Expense		510	150	00		
		Cash	Ck 3	110			150	00
	6	Accounts Payable		210	6150	00		
		Cash	Ck 4	110			6150	00
	12	Cash		110	1000	00		
		Sales	T13	410			1000	00
	16	Art Kline, Drawing		320	600	00		
		Cash	Ck 5	110			600	00

Account Title: *Cash* — **Account No.** 110

Date 20—		Explanation	Post. Ref.	Debit		Credit		Balance Debit		Balance Credit	
Jan.	1		J1	15000	00			15000	00		
	2		J1	1500	00			16500	00		
	5		J1			150	00	16350	00		
	6		J1			6150	00	10200	00		
	12		J1	1000	00			11200	00		
	16		J1			600	00	10600	00		

2.1 (cont'd)

Account Title: *Accounts Payable*   **Account No.** 210

Date 20—		Explanation	Post. Ref.	Debit		Credit		Balance			
								Debit		Credit	
Jan.		Balance Brought Forward	✔							6150	00
	6		J1	6150	00					—	

Account Title: *Art Kline, Capital*   **Account No.** 310

Date 20—		Explanation	Post. Ref.	Debit		Credit		Balance			
								Debit		Credit	
Jan.	1		J1			15000	00			15000	00

Account Title: *Art Kline, Drawing*   **Account No.** 320

Date 20—		Explanation	Post. Ref.	Debit		Credit		Balance			
								Debit		Credit	
Jan.	16		J1	600	00			600	00		

Account Title: *Sales*   **Account No.** 410

Date 20—		Explanation	Post. Ref.	Debit		Credit		Balance			
								Debit		Credit	
Jan.	2		J1			1500	00			1500	00
	12		J1			1000	00			2500	00

Account Title: *Advertising Expense*   **Account No.** 510

Date 20—		Explanation	Post. Ref.	Debit		Credit		Balance			
								Debit		Credit	
Jan.	5		J1	150	00			150	00		

2.2–2.5

JOURNAL							Page 1	
Date 20—	Account Title and Explanation	Doc No.	Post. Ref.	General Debit			General Credit	
June 1	Cash		110	1400	00			
	Accounts Receivable		120	600	00			
	Supplies		130	1400	00			
	Prepaid Insurance		140	500	00			
	Equipment		150	2600	00			
	Accounts Payable		210				1100	00
	Notes Payable		220				700	00
	Buford Burke, Capital	M1	310				4700	00
5	Cash		110	1500	00			
	Buford Burke, Capital	R2	310				1500	00
6	Prepaid Insurance		140	150	00			
	Cash	Ck1	110				150	00
8	Supplies		130	75	00			
	Cash	Ck2	110				75	00
10	Equipment		150	100	00			
	Accounts Payable	P2	210				100	00
10	Cash		110	890	00			
	Sales	T2	410				890	00
12	Accounts Payable		210	125	00			
	Cash	Ck3	110				125	00
13	Notes Payable		220	150	00			
	Cash	Ck4	110				150	00
17	Cash		110	1625	00			
	Sales	T3	410				1625	00
19	Rent Expense		510	350	00			
	Cash	Ck5	110				350	00
22	Buford Burke, Drawing		320	600	00			
	Cash	Ck6	110				600	00
23	Cash		110	200	00			
	Accounts Receivable	R3	120				200	00

2.2–2.5 (cont'd)

Account Title: *Cash*   **Account No.** *110*

Date 20—		Explanation	Post. Ref.	Debit		Credit		Balance Debit		Credit	
June	1	Opening entry	J1	1400	00			1400	00		
	5		J1	1500	00			2900	00		
	6		J1			150	00	2750	00		
	8		J1			75	00	2675	00		
	10		J1	890	00			3565	00		
	12		J1			125	00	3440	00		
	13		J1			150	00	3290	00		
	17		J1	1625	00			4915	00		
	19		J1			350	00	4565	00		
	22		J1			600	00	3965	00		
	23		J1	200	00			4165	00		

Account Title: *Accounts Receivable*   **Account No.** *120*

Date 20—		Explanation	Post. Ref.	Debit		Credit		Balance Debit		Credit	
June	1	Opening entry	J1	600	00			600	00		
	23		J1			200	00	400	00		

Account Title: *Supplies*   **Account No.** *130*

Date 20—		Explanation	Post. Ref.	Debit		Credit		Balance Debit		Credit	
June	1	Opening entry	J1	1400	00			1400	00		
	8		J1	75	00			1475	00		

2.2–2.5   (cont'd)

Account Title: *Prepaid Insurance*								Account No. *140*	
Date 20—		Explanation	Post. Ref.	Debit		Credit		Balance	
								Debit	Credit
June	1	Opening entry	J1	500	00			500	00		
	6		J1	150	00			650	00		

Account Title: *Equipment*								Account No. *150*	
Date 20—		Explanation	Post. Ref.	Debit		Credit		Balance	
								Debit	Credit
June	1	Opening entry	J1	2600	00			2600	00		
	10		J1	100	00			2700	00		

Account Title: *Accounts Payable*								Account No. *210*	
Date 20—		Explanation	Post. Ref.	Debit		Credit		Balance	
								Debit	Credit
June	1	Opening entry	J1			1100	00			1100	00
	10		J1			100	00			1200	00
	12		J1	125	00					1075	00

Account Title: *Notes Payable*								Account No. *220*	
Date 20—		Explanation	Post. Ref.	Debit		Credit		Balance	
								Debit	Credit
June	1	Opening entry	J1			700	00			700	00
	13		J1	150	00					550	00

Account Title: *Buford Burke, Capital*								Account No. *310*	
Date 20—		Explanation	Post. Ref.	Debit		Credit		Balance	
								Debit	Credit
June	1	Opening entry	J1			4700	00			4700	00
	5		J1			1500	00			6200	00

2.2–2.5 (cont'd)

Account Title: *Buford Burke, Drawing*									Account No. *320*			

Account Title: *Buford Burke, Drawing* **Account No. *320***

Date 20—		Explanation	Post. Ref.	Debit		Credit		Balance				
								Debit		Credit		
June	22		*J1*	600	00			600	00			

Account Title: *Sales* **Account No. *410***

Date 20—		Explanation	Post. Ref.	Debit		Credit		Balance				
								Debit		Credit		
June	10		*J1*			890	00			890	00	
	17		*J1*			1625	00			2515	00	

Account Title: *Rent Expense* **Account No. *510***

Date 20—		Explanation	Post. Ref.	Debit		Credit		Balance				
								Debit		Credit		
June	19		*J1*	350	00			350	00			

2.6 a. $4,165.00

    b. $4,165.00

SECTION III

3.1

JOURNAL								Page /
Date 20—		Account Title and Explanation	Doc No.	Post. Ref.	General Debit		General Credit	
Jan.	1	Cash		110	15000	00		
		Art Kline, Capital	M1	310			15000	00
	1	Supplies		130	6150	00		
		Main's Supply Co.	P2	210			6150	00
	2	Cash		110	1500	00		
		Sales	I2	410			1500	00
	3	Equipment		150	8110	00		
		Office Max	P3	220			8110	00
	3	Rent Expense		530	950	00		
		Cash	Ck 1	110			950	00
	5	Petty Cash		120	200	00		
		Cash	Ck 2	110			200	00
	5	Cash		110	1000	00		
		Sales	I5	410			1000	00
	11	Miscellaneous Expense		520	55	00		
		Cash	Ck 3	110			55	00
	11	Repair Expense		540	890	00		
		Mike's Garage	M4	230			890	00
	14	Advertising Expense		510	150	00		
		Cash	Ck 4	110			150	00
	15	Miscellaneous Expense		520	80	00		
		Cash	Ck 5	110			80	00
	15	Main's Supply Co.		210	6150	00		
		Cash	Ck 6	110			6150	00
	17	Utilities Expense		560	980	00		
		Cash	Ck 7	110			980	00

3.1 (cont'd)

JOURNAL								Page 2	
Date 20—		Account Title and Explanation	Doc No.	Post. Ref.	General Debit		General Credit		
Jan.	18	Cash		110	2500	00			
		Sales	I18	410			2500	00	
	18	Office Max		220	2000	00			
		Cash	Ck 8	110			2000	00	
	19	Prepaid Insurance		140	1150	00			
		Cash	Ck 9	110			1150	00	
	20	Art Kline, Drawing		320	1500	00			
		Cash	Ck 10	110			1500	00	

Account Title: *Cash*								Account No. *110*			
Date 20—		Explanation	Post. Ref.	Debit		Credit		Balance			
								Debit		Credit	
Jan.	*1*		J1	15000	00			15000	00		
	2		J1	1500	00			16500	00		
	3		J1			950	00	15550	00		
	5		J1			200	00	15350	00		
	5		J1	1000	00			16350	00		
	11		J1			55	00	16295	00		
	14		J1			150	00	16145	00		
	15		J1			80	00	16065	00		
	15		J1			6150	00	9915	00		
	17		J1			980	00	8935	00		
	18		J2	2500	00			11435	00		
	18		J2			2000	00	9435	00		
	19		J2			1150	00	8285	00		
	20		J2			1500	00	6785	00		

3.1 (cont'd)

Account Title: Petty Cash

Account No. 120

Date 20—		Explanation	Post. Ref.	Debit		Credit		Balance Debit		Balance Credit	
Jan.	5		J1	200	00			200	00		

Account Title: Supplies

Account No. 130

Date 20—		Explanation	Post. Ref.	Debit		Credit		Balance Debit		Balance Credit	
Jan.	1		J1	6150	00			6150	00		

Account Title: Prepaid Insurance

Account No. 140

Date 20—		Explanation	Post. Ref.	Debit		Credit		Balance Debit		Balance Credit	
Jan.	19		J2	1150	00			1150	00		

Account Title: Equipment

Account No. 150

Date 20—		Explanation	Post. Ref.	Debit		Credit		Balance Debit		Balance Credit	
Jan.	3		J1	8110	00			8110	00		

Account Title: Main's Supply Co.

Account No. 210

Date 20—		Explanation	Post. Ref.	Debit		Credit		Balance Debit		Balance Credit	
Jan.	1		J1			6150	00			6150	00
	15		J1	6150	00						

3.1 (cont'd)

Account Title: *Office Max* **Account No.** *220*

Date 20—		Explanation	Post. Ref.	Debit		Credit		Balance			
								Debit		Credit	
Jan.	3		J1			8110	00			8110	00
	18		J2	2000	00					6110	00

Account Title: *Mike's Garage* **Account No.** *230*

Date 20—		Explanation	Post. Ref.	Debit		Credit		Balance			
								Debit		Credit	
Jan.	11		J1			890	00			890	00

Account Title: *Art Kline, Capital* **Account No.** *310*

Date 20—		Explanation	Post. Ref.	Debit		Credit		Balance			
								Debit		Credit	
Jan.	1		J1			15000	00			15000	00

Account Title: *Art Kline, Drawing* **Account No.** *320*

Date 20—		Explanation	Post. Ref.	Debit		Credit		Balance			
								Debit		Credit	
Jan.	20		J2	1500	00			1500	00		

Account Title: *Sales* **Account No.** *410*

Date 20—		Explanation	Post. Ref.	Debit		Credit		Balance			
								Debit		Credit	
Jan.	2		J1			1500	00			1500	00
	5		J1			1000	00			2500	00
	18		J2			2500	00			5000	00

Accounting LIFEPAC 4

3.1 (cont'd)

Account Title: *Advertising Expense* Account No. 510

Date 20—		Explanation	Post. Ref.	Debit		Credit		Balance Debit		Credit	
Jan.	14		J1	150	00			150	00		

Account Title: *Miscellaneous Expense* Account No. 520

Date 20—		Explanation	Post. Ref.	Debit		Credit		Balance Debit		Credit	
Jan.	11		J1	55	00			55	00		
	15		J1	80	00			135	00		

Account Title: *Rent Expense* Account No. 530

Date 20—		Explanation	Post. Ref.	Debit		Credit		Balance Debit		Credit	
Jan.	3		J1	950	00			950	00		

Account Title: *Repair Expense* Account No. 540

Date 20—		Explanation	Post. Ref.	Debit		Credit		Balance Debit		Credit	
Jan.	11		J1	890	00			890	00		

Account Title: *Supplies Expense* Account No. 550

Date		Explanation	Post. Ref.	Debit		Credit		Balance Debit		Credit	

3.1 (cont'd)

Account Title: *Utilities Expense*										Account No. *560*		
Date		Explanation	Post. Ref.	Debit		Credit		Balance				
20—								Debit			Credit	
Jan.	*17*		*J1*	*980*	*00*			*980*	*00*			

3.2 ***Teacher's Note*** – The practice of listing accounts with zero balances on the trial balance is observed in this LIFEPAC only. Subsequent LIFEPACs will not require that this be done.

Kline's Cleaning Service						
Trial Balance						
January 20, 20—						
ACCOUNT TITLE		ACCT. NO.	DEBIT		CREDIT	
Cash		*110*	*6785*	*00*		
Petty Cash		*120*	*200*	*00*		
Supplies		*130*	*6150*	*00*		
Prepaid Insurance		*140*	*1150*	*00*		
Equipment		*150*	*8110*	*00*		
Main's Supply Co.		*210*				
Office Max		*220*			*6110*	*00*
Mike's Garage		*230*			*890*	*00*
Art Kline, Capital		*310*			*15000*	*00*
Art Kline, Drawing		*320*	*1500*	*00*		
Sales		*410*			*5000*	*00*
Advertising Expense		*510*	*150*	*00*		
Miscellaneous Expense		*520*	*135*	*00*		
Rent Expense		*530*	*950*	*00*		
Repair Expense		*540*	*890*	*00*		
Supplies Expense		*550*				
Utilities Expense		*560*	*980*	*00*		
Totals			*27000*	*00*	*27000*	*00*

SECTION IV

4.1–4.2

		JOURNAL					Page /	
Date 20—		Account Title and Explanation	Doc No.	Post. Ref.	General Debit		General Credit	
May	1	Cash		110	14500	00		
		Don Levy, Capital	R1	310			14500	00
	3	Prepaid Insurance		130	1350	00		
		Cash	Ck 1	110			1350	00
	5	Supplies		120	1400	00		
		Snapp's Supply	P1	210			1400	00
	5	Rent Expense		530	950	00		
		Cash	Ck 2	110			950	00
	7	Miscellaneous Expense		520	5	00		
		Cash	Ck 3	110			5	00
	8	Supplies		120	1050	00		
		Cash	Ck 4	110			1050	00
	8	Cash		110	1650	00		
		Sales	T8	410			1650	00
	9	Snapp's Supply		210	1400	00		
		Cash	Ck 5	110			1400	00
	10	Repair Expense		540	85	00		
		Cash	Ck 6	110			85	00
	11	Advertising Expense		510	110	00		
		Cash	Ck 7	110			110	00
	12	Cash		110	1150	00		
		Sales	T12	410			1150	00
	14	Utilities Expense		550	75	00		
		Cash	Ck 8	110			75	00
	14	Cash		110	550	00		
		Sales	T14	410			550	00
	15	Don Levy, Drawing		320	450	00		
		Cash	Ck 9	110			450	00
	16	Cash		110	675	00		
		Sales	T16	410			675	00

4.1–4.2

| Account Title: *Cash* | | | | | | | | Account No. *110* | | |

Date 20—		Explanation	Post. Ref.	Debit		Credit		Balance			
								Debit		Credit	
May	*1*		*J1*	14500	00			14500	00		
	3		*J1*			1350	00	13150	00		
	5		*J1*			950	00	12200	00		
	7		*J1*			5	00	12195	00		
	8		*J1*			1050	00	11145	00		
	8		*J1*	1650	00			12795	00		
	9		*J1*			1400	00	11395	00		
	10		*J1*			85	00	11310	00		
	11		*J1*			110	00	11200	00		
	12		*J1*	1150	00			12350	00		
	14		*J1*			75	00	12275	00		
	14		*J1*	550	00			12825	00		
	15		*J1*			450	00	12375	00		
	16		*J1*	675	00			13050	00		

| Account Title: *Supplies* | | | | | | | | Account No. *120* | | |

Date 20—		Explanation	Post. Ref.	Debit		Credit		Balance			
								Debit		Credit	
May	*5*		*J1*	1400	00			1400	00		
	8		*J1*	1050	00			2450	00		

| Account Title: *Prepaid Insurance* | | | | | | | | Account No. *130* | | |

Date 20—		Explanation	Post. Ref.	Debit		Credit		Balance			
								Debit		Credit	
May	*3*		*J1*	1350	00			1350	00		

4.1–4.2

Account Title: *Snapp's Supply*								Account No. *210*			
Date 20—		Explanation	Post. Ref.	Debit		Credit		Balance			
								Debit		Credit	
May	5		*J1*			1400	00			1400	00
	9		*J1*	1400	00					———	

Account Title: *Don Levy, Capital*								Account No. *310*			
Date 20—		Explanation	Post. Ref.	Debit		Credit		Balance			
								Debit		Credit	
May	1		*J1*			14500	00			14500	00

Account Title: *Don Levy, Drawing*								Account No. *320*			
Date 20—		Explanation	Post. Ref.	Debit		Credit		Balance			
								Debit		Credit	
May	15		*J1*	450	00			450	00		

Account Title: *Sales*								Account No. *410*			
Date 20—		Explanation	Post. Ref.	Debit		Credit		Balance			
								Debit		Credit	
May	8		*J1*			1650	00			1650	00
	12		*J1*			1150	00			2800	00
	14		*J1*			550	00			3350	00
	16		*J1*			675	00			4025	00

4.1–4.2

Account Title: *Advertising Expense*								Account No. *510*	
Date 20—		Explanation	Post. Ref.	Debit		Credit		Balance	
								Debit	Credit
May	*11*		*J1*	110	00			110	00	

Account Title: *Miscellaneous Expense*								Account No. *520*	
Date 20—		Explanation	Post. Ref.	Debit		Credit		Balance	
								Debit	Credit
May	*7*		*J1*	5	00			5	00	

Account Title: *Rent Expense*								Account No. *530*	
Date 20—		Explanation	Post. Ref.	Debit		Credit		Balance	
								Debit	Credit
May	*5*		*J1*	950	00			950	00	

Account Title: *Repair Expense*								Account No. *540*	
Date 20—		Explanation	Post. Ref.	Debit		Credit		Balance	
								Debit	Credit
May	*10*		*J1*	85	00			85	00	

Account Title: *Utilities Expense*								Account No. *550*	
Date 20—		Explanation	Post. Ref.	Debit		Credit		Balance	
								Debit	Credit
May	*14*		*J1*	75	00			75	00	

4.3 a. $13,050.00

b. $13,050.00

4.4

Pet-A-Care Chart of Accounts			
Balance Sheet		**Income Statement**	
Assets		*Revenue*	
Cash	110	Grooming Fees	410
Supplies	120		
Prepaid Insurance	130	*Expenses*	
Office Equipment	140	Advertising Expense	510
		Miscellaneous Expense	520
Liabilities		Rent Expense	530
Office Max	210	Repair Expense	540
West's Grooming Supplies	220	Salary Expense	550
		Utilities Expense	560
Capital			
Tammy Jennings, Capital	310		
Tammy Jennings, Drawing	320		

4.5

		JOURNAL							**Page**	/
Date 20—		**Account Title and Explanation**	**Doc No.**	**Post. Ref.**	**General Debit**			**General Credit**		
June	1	Cash		110	20000	00				
		Tammy Jennings, Capital	R1	310				20000	00	
	2	Rent Expense		530	900	00				
		Cash	Ck 1	110				900	00	
	3	Supplies		120	1600	00				
		Cash	Ck 2	110				1600	00	
	4	Office Equipment		140	18000	00				
		Office Max	P1	210				18000	00	
	5	Prepaid Insurance		130	600	00				
		Cash	Ck 3	110				600	00	
	5	Cash		110	1900	00				
		Grooming Fees	T5	410				1900	00	
	8	Office Max		210	1200	00				
		Cash	Ck 4	110				1200	00	
	9	Repair Expense		540	65	00				
		Cash	Ck 5	110				65	00	
	9	Salary Expense		550	789	00				
		Cash	Ck 6	110				789	00	
	10	Supplies		120	1300	00				
		West's Grooming Supplies	P2	220				1300	00	
	10	Advertising Expense		510	75	00				
		Cash	Ck 7	110				75	00	
	11	Tammy Jennings, Drawing		320	450	00				
		Cash	Ck 8	110				450	00	
	12	Supplies		120	980	00				
		Cash	Ck 9	110				980	00	

4.5 (cont'd)

JOURNAL								Page 2
Date 20—	Account Title and Explanation	Doc No.	Post. Ref.	General Debit		General Credit		
June 13	Cash		110	3450	00			
	Grooming Fees	I13	410			3450	00	
13	Supplies		120	850	00			
	West's Grooming Supplies	P3	220			850	00	
14	Salary Expense		550	989	00			
	Cash	Ck 10	110			989	00	
15	Office Max		210	1200	00			
	Cash	Ck 11	110			1200	00	
16	Cash		110	3590	00			
	Grooming Fees	I16	410			3590	00	
19	West's Grooming Supplies		220	1300	00			
	Cash	Ck 12	110			1300	00	
20	Prepaid Insurance		130	1250	00			
	Cash	Ck 13	110			1250	00	
22	Advertising Expense		510	85	00			
	Cash	Ck 14	110			85	00	
23	Tammy Jennings, Drawing		320	550	00			
	Cash	Ck 15	110			550	00	
30	Salary Expense		550	780	00			
	Cash	Ck 16	110			780	00	
30	Utilities Expense		560	656	00			
	Cash	Ck 17	110			656	00	
30	Miscellaneous Expense		520	92	00			
	Cash	Ck 18	110			92	00	

4.6

Account Title: *Cash* — Account No. *110*

Date 20—		Explanation	Post. Ref.	Debit		Credit		Balance Debit		Balance Credit	
June	1		J1	20000	00			20000	00		
	2		J1			900	00	19100	00		
	3		J1			1600	00	17500	00		
	5		J1			600	00	16900	00		
	5		J1	1900	00			18800	00		
	8		J1			1200	00	17600	00		
	9		J1			65	00	17535	00		
	9		J1			789	00	16746	00		
	10		J1			75	00	16671	00		
	11		J1			450	00	16221	00		
	12		J1			980	00	15421	00		
	13		J2	3450	00			18691	00		
	14		J2			989	00	17702	00		
	15		J2			1200	00	16502	00		
	16		J2	3590	00			20092	00		
	19		J2			1300	00	18792	00		
	20		J2			1250	00	17542	00		
	22		J2			85	00	17457	00		
	23		J2			550	00	16907	00		
	30		J2			780	00	16127	00		
	30		J2			656	00	15471	00		
	30		J2			92	00	15379	00		

Account Title: *Supplies* — Account No. *120*

Date 20—		Explanation	Post. Ref.	Debit		Credit		Balance Debit		Balance Credit	
June	3		J1	1600	00			1600	00		
	10		J1	1300	00			2900	00		
	12		J1	980	00			3880	00		
	13		J2	850	00			4730	00		

4.6 (cont'd)

Account Title: *Prepaid Insurance*   **Account No. 130**

Date 20—		Explanation	Post. Ref.	Debit		Credit		Balance Debit		Credit	
June	5		J1	600	00			600	00		
	20		J2	1250	00			1850	00		

Account Title: *Office Equipment*   **Account No. 140**

Date 20—		Explanation	Post. Ref.	Debit		Credit		Balance Debit		Credit	
June	4		J1	18000	00			18000	00		

Account Title: *Office Max*   **Account No. 210**

Date 20—		Explanation	Post. Ref.	Debit		Credit		Balance Debit		Credit	
June	4		J1			18000	00			18000	00
	8		J1	1200	00					16800	00
	15		J2	1200	00					15600	00

Account Title: *West's Grooming Supplies*   **Account No. 220**

Date 20—		Explanation	Post. Ref.	Debit		Credit		Balance Debit		Credit	
June	10		J1			1300	00			1300	00
	13		J2			850	00			2150	00
	19		J2	1300	00					850	00

4.6 (cont'd)

Account Title: *Tammy Jennings, Capital*								Account No. *310*	
Date 20—		Explanation	Post. Ref.	Debit		Credit		Balance	
								Debit	Credit
June	*1*		*J1*			20000	00		20000	00

Account Title: *Tammy Jennings, Drawing*								Account No. *320*	
Date 20—		Explanation	Post. Ref.	Debit		Credit		Balance	
								Debit	Credit
June	*11*		*J1*	450	00			450	00	
	23		*J2*	550	00			1000	00	

Account Title: *Grooming Fees*								Account No. *410*	
Date 20—		Explanation	Post. Ref.	Debit		Credit		Balance	
								Debit	Credit
June	*5*		*J1*			1900	00		1900	00
	13		*J2*			3450	00		5350	00
	16		*J2*			3590	00		8940	00

Account Title: *Advertising Expense*								Account No. *510*	
Date 20—		Explanation	Post. Ref.	Debit		Credit		Balance	
								Debit	Credit
June	*10*		*J1*	75	00			75	00	
	22		*J2*	85	00			160	00	

4.6 (cont'd)

Account Title: *Miscellaneous Expense*								Account No. *520*		
Date 20—		Explanation	Post. Ref.	Debit		Credit		Balance		
								Debit		Credit
June	30		J2	92	00			92	00	

Account Title: *Rent Expense*								Account No. *530*		
Date 20—		Explanation	Post. Ref.	Debit		Credit		Balance		
								Debit		Credit
June	2		J1	900	00			900	00	

Account Title: *Repair Expense*								Account No. *540*		
Date 20—		Explanation	Post. Ref.	Debit		Credit		Balance		
								Debit		Credit
June	9		J1	65	00			65	00	

Account Title: *Salary Expense*								Account No. *550*		
Date 20—		Explanation	Post. Ref.	Debit		Credit		Balance		
								Debit		Credit
June	9		J1	789	00			789	00	
	14		J2	989	00			1778	00	
	30		J2	780	00			2558	00	

4.6 (cont'd)

Account Title: *Utilities Expense*							Account No. *560*			
Date 20—		Explanation	Post. Ref.	Debit		Credit		Balance		
								Debit		Credit
June	30		*J2*	656	00			656	00	

4.7 a. $15,379.00

    b. $15,379.00

4.8

Pet-A-Care					
Trial Balance					
June 30, 20—					
ACCOUNT TITLE	ACCT. NO.	DEBIT		CREDIT	
Cash	*110*	15379	00		
Supplies	*120*	4730	00		
Prepaid Insurance	*130*	1850	00		
Equipment	*140*	18000	00		
Office Max	*210*			15600	00
West's Grooming Supplies	*220*			850	00
Tammy Jennings, Capital	*310*			20000	00
Tammy Jennings, Drawing	*320*	1000	00		
Grooming Fees	*410*			8940	00
Advertising Expense	*510*	160	00		
Miscellaneous Expense	*520*	92	00		
Rent Expense	*530*	900	00		
Repair Expense	*540*	65	00		
Salary Expense	*550*	2558	00		
Utilities Expense	*560*	656	00		
Totals		45390	00	45390	00

4.9

		JOURNAL							Page *1*
Date 20—		Account Title and Explanation	Doc No.	Post. Ref.	General Debit			General Credit	
June	*1*	*Cash*		*110*	*4000*	*00*			
		Wilma Poole, Capital	*R1*	*310*				*4000*	*00*
	2	*Rent Expense*		*530*	*1900*	*00*			
		Cash	*Ck1*	*110*				*1900*	*00*
	3	*Supplies*		*120*	*1200*	*00*			
		Cash	*Ck2*	*110*				*1200*	*00*
	4	*Office Equipment*		*140*	*1100*	*00*			
		Wilson's Supply	*P1*	*220*				*1100*	*00*
	5	*Prepaid Insurance*		*130*	*2600*	*00*			
		Cash	*Ck3*	*110*				*2600*	*00*
	5	*Cash*		*110*	*2980*	*00*			
		Repair Fees	*T5*	*410*				*2980*	*00*
	8	*Wilson's Supply*		*220*	*1000*	*00*			
		Cash	*Ck4*	*110*				*1000*	*00*
	9	*Repair Expense*		*540*	*195*	*00*			
		Cash	*Ck5*	*110*				*195*	*00*
	9	*Salary Expense*		*550*	*1789*	*00*			
		Cash	*Ck6*	*110*				*1789*	*00*
	10	*Supplies*		*120*	*1440*	*00*			
		Gold 'n Things	*P2*	*210*				*1440*	*00*
	10	*Advertising Expense*		*510*	*195*	*00*			
		Cash	*Ck7*	*110*				*195*	*00*
	11	*Wilma Poole, Drawing*		*320*	*950*	*00*			
		Cash	*Ck8*	*110*				*950*	*00*

4.10

		JOURNAL						Page *2*	
Date 20—		Account Title and Explanation	Doc No.	Post. Ref.	General Debit		General Credit		
June	*12*	*Miscellaneous Expense*		*520*	*80*	*00*			
		Cash	*Ck9*	*110*			*80*	*00*	
	13	*Cash*		*110*	*3950*	*00*			
		Repair Fees	*T13*	*410*			*3950*	*00*	
	13	*Supplies*		*120*	*1800*	*00*			
		Wilson's Supply	*P3*	*220*			*1800*	*00*	
	14	*Salary Expense*		*550*	*1789*	*00*			
		Cash	*Ck10*	*110*			*1789*	*00*	
	15	*Gold 'n Things*		*210*	*600*	*00*			
		Cash	*Ck11*	*110*			*600*	*00*	
	16	*Cash*		*110*	*2190*	*00*			
		Repair Fees	*T16*	*410*			*2190*	*00*	
	20	*Prepaid Insurance*		*130*	*1410*	*00*			
		Cash	*Ck12*	*110*			*1410*	*00*	
	22	*Advertising Expense*		*510*	*285*	*00*			
		Cash	*Ck13*	*110*			*285*	*00*	
	23	*Wilma Poole, Drawing*		*320*	*650*	*00*			
		Cash	*Ck14*	*110*			*650*	*00*	
	30	*Salary Expense*		*550*	*1789*	*00*			
		Cash	*Ck15*	*110*			*1789*	*00*	
	30	*Utilities Expense*		*560*	*560*	*00*			
		Cash	*Ck16*	*110*			*560*	*00*	

4.11

Account Title: Cash							Account No. 110		

Date 20—		Explanation	Post. Ref.	Debit		Credit		Balance	
								Debit	Credit
June	1	Opening entry	J1	5000	00			5000	00	
	1		J1	4000	00			9000	00	
	2		J1			1900	00	7100	00	
	3		J1			1200	00	5900	00	
	5		J1			2600	00	3300	00	
	5		J1	2980	00			6280	00	
	8		J1			1000	00	5280	00	
	9		J1			195	00	5085	00	
	9		J1			1789	00	3296	00	
	10		J1			195	00	3101	00	
	11		J1			950	00	2151	00	
	12		J2			80	00	2071	00	
	13		J2	3950	00			6021	00	
	14		J2			1789	00	4232	00	
	15		J2			600	00	3632	00	
	16		J2	2190	00			5822	00	
	20		J2			1410	00	4412	00	
	22		J2			285	00	4127	00	
	23		J2			650	00	3477	00	
	30		J2			1789	00	1688	00	
	30		J2			560	00	1128	00	

Account Title: Supplies							Account No. 120		

Date 20—		Explanation	Post. Ref.	Debit		Credit		Balance	
								Debit	Credit
June	1	Opening entry	J1	600	00			600	00	
	3		J1	1200	00			1800	00	
	10		J1	1440	00			3240	00	
	13		J2	1800	00			5040	00	

4.11 (cont'd)

Account Title: *Prepaid Insurance*						Account No. *130*			
Date 20—		Explanation	Post. Ref.	Debit		Credit		Balance	
								Debit	Credit
June	1	Opening entry	J1	800	00			800	00		
	5		J1	2600	00			3400	00		
	20		J2	1410	00			4810	00		

Account Title: *Office Equipment*						Account No. *140*			
Date 20—		Explanation	Post. Ref.	Debit		Credit		Balance	
								Debit	Credit
June	1	Opening entry	J1	6000	00			6000	00		
	4		J1	1100	00			7100	00		

Account Title: *Gold 'n Things*						Account No. *210*			
Date 20—		Explanation	Post. Ref.	Debit		Credit		Balance	
								Debit	Credit
June	1	Opening entry	J1			600	00			600	00
	10		J1			1440	00			2040	00
	15		J2	600	00					1440	00

Account Title: *Wilson's Supply*						Account No. *220*			
Date 20—		Explanation	Post. Ref.	Debit		Credit		Balance	
								Debit	Credit
June	1	Opening entry	J1			2000	00			2000	00
	4		J1			1100	00			3100	00
	8		J1	1000	00					2100	00
	13		J2			1800	00			3900	00

4.11 (cont'd)

Account Title: *Wilma Poole, Capital*   **Account No.** *310*

Date 20—		Explanation	Post. Ref.	Debit		Credit		Balance			
								Debit		Credit	
June	1	Opening entry	J1			9800	00			9800	00
	1		J1			4000	00			13800	00

Account Title: *Wilma Poole, Drawing*   **Account No.** *320*

Date 20—		Explanation	Post. Ref.	Debit		Credit		Balance			
								Debit		Credit	
June	11		J1	950	00			950	00		
	23		J2	650	00			1600	00		

Account Title: *Repair Fees*   **Account No.** *410*

Date 20—		Explanation	Post. Ref.	Debit		Credit		Balance			
								Debit		Credit	
June	5		J1			2980	00			2980	00
	13		J2			3950	00			6930	00
	16		J2			2190	00			9120	00

Account Title: *Advertising Expense*   **Account No.** *510*

Date 20—		Explanation	Post. Ref.	Debit		Credit		Balance			
								Debit		Credit	
June	10		J1	195	00			195	00		
	22		J2	285	00			480	00		

4.11 (cont'd)

Account Title: Miscellaneous Expense					Account No. 520		
Date 20—	Explanation	Post. Ref.	Debit	Credit	Balance		
					Debit	Credit	
June 12		J2	80 00		80 00		

Account Title: Rent Expense					Account No. 530		
Date 20—	Explanation	Post. Ref.	Debit	Credit	Balance		
					Debit	Credit	
June 2		J1	1900 00		1900 00		

Account Title: Repair Expense					Account No. 540		
Date 20—	Explanation	Post. Ref.	Debit	Credit	Balance		
					Debit	Credit	
June 9		J1	195 00		195 00		

Account Title: Salary Expense					Account No. 550		
Date 20—	Explanation	Post. Ref.	Debit	Credit	Balance		
					Debit	Credit	
June 9		J1	1789 00		1789 00		
14		J2	1789 00		3578 00		
30		J2	1789 00		5367 00		

4.11 (cont'd)

Account Title: Utilities Expense								Account No. 560		
Date 20—		Explanation	Post. Ref.	Debit		Credit		Balance Debit		Credit
June	30		J2	560	00			560	00	

4.12

Poole's Gold
Trial Balance
June 30, 20—

ACCOUNT TITLE	ACCT. NO.	DEBIT		CREDIT	
Cash	110	1128	00		
Supplies	120	5040	00		
Prepaid Insurance	130	4810	00		
Office Equipment	140	7100	00		
Gold 'n Things	210			1440	00
Wilson's Supply	220			3900	00
Wilma Poole, Capital	310			13800	00
Wilma Poole, Drawing	320	1600	00		
Repair Fees	410			9120	00
Advertising Expense	510	480	00		
Miscellaneous Expense	520	80	00		
Rent Expense	530	1900	00		
Repair Expense	540	195	00		
Salary Expense	550	5367	00		
Utilities Expense	560	560	00		
Totals		28260	00	28260	00

OPTIONAL EXERCISES FOR EXTRA CREDIT

*Teacher's Note: Each item in the journal below counts as **one-half** point, including the page number, the year, the month and the day of the month. All amounts, account titles, document numbers and account numbers count as single items. This problem has 84 individual items. **Total Points – 42***

JOURNAL					Page 5			
Date 20—		Account Title and Explanation	Doc No.	Post. Ref.	General Debit		General Credit	
Apr.	1	Office Equipment		130	18000	00		
		James Carlson, Capital	M1	310			18000	00
	2	Building		160	85000	00		
		Mortgage Payable		220			68000	00
		Cash	Ck100	110			17000	00
	3	Office Supplies		120	75	00		
		Accounts Payable	P2	210			75	00
	4	Delivery Truck		150	7500	00		
		Cash	Ck101	110			7500	00
	5	Salary Expense		540	500	00		
		Cash	Ck102	110			500	00
	6	Cash		110	9200	00		
		Service Fees	T6	410			9200	00
	7	Advertising Expense		510	250	00		
		Cash	Ck103	110			250	00
	8	Accounts Payable		210	75	00		
		Cash	Ck104	110			75	00
	9	Repair Equipment		140	840	00		
		Accounts Payable	P3	210			840	00
	10	Rent Expense		530	1200	00		
		Cash	Ck105	110			1200	00

*Teacher's Note: Each item in the ledger accounts on the following pages counts as **one-half** point, including the account title, account number, year, month, day, posting reference number and correct debit or credit amounts. Points are listed underneath each ledger account.*

Account Title: *Cash*   **Account No.** *110*

Date 20—		Explanation	Post. Ref.	Debit		Credit		Balance Debit		Credit	
Apr.	1	Balance Brought Fwd.	✔					50000	00		
	2		J5			17000	00	33000	00		
	4		J5			7500	00	25500	00		
	5		J5			500	00	25000	00		
	6		J5	9200	00			34200	00		
	7		J5			250	00	33950	00		
	8		J5			75	00	33875	00		
	10		J5			1200	00	32675	00		

Total Points – 18

Account Title: *Office Supplies*   **Account No.** *120*

Date 20—		Explanation	Post. Ref.	Debit		Credit		Balance Debit		Credit	
Apr.	1	Balance Brought Fwd.	✔					1200	00		
	3		J5	75	00			1275	00		

Total Points – 6

Account Title: *Office Equipment*   **Account No.** *130*

Date 20—		Explanation	Post. Ref.	Debit		Credit		Balance Debit		Credit	
Apr.	1		J5	18000	00			18000	00		

Total Points – 4

Account Title: *Repair Equipment*   **Account No.** *140*

Date 20—		Explanation	Post. Ref.	Debit		Credit		Balance Debit		Credit	
Apr.	1	Balance Brought Fwd.	✔					6000	00		
	9		J5	840	00			6840	00		

Total Points – 6

Account Title: *Delivery Truck*   Account No. *150*

Date 20—		Explanation	Post. Ref.	Debit		Credit		Balance			
								Debit		Credit	
Apr.	*4*		*J5*	7500	00			7500	00		

Total Points – 4

Account Title: *Building*   Account No. *160*

Date 20—		Explanation	Post. Ref.	Debit		Credit		Balance			
								Debit		Credit	
Apr.	*2*		*J5*	85000	00			85000	00		

Total Points – 4

Account Title: *Land*   Account No. *170*

Date 20—		Explanation	Post. Ref.	Debit		Credit		Balance			
								Debit		Credit	
Apr.	*1*	*Balance Brought Fwd.*	✔					60000	00		

Total Points – 4

Account Title: *Accounts Payable*   Account No. *210*

Date 20—		Explanation	Post. Ref.	Debit		Credit		Balance			
								Debit		Credit	
Apr.	*3*		*J5*			75	00			75	00
	8		*J5*	75	00					—	
	9		*J5*			840	00			840	00

Total Points – 8

Account Title: *Mortgage Payable*   Account No. *220*

Date 20—		Explanation	Post. Ref.	Debit		Credit		Balance			
								Debit		Credit	
Apr.	*2*		*J5*			68000	00			68000	00

Total Points – 4

Account Title: James Carlson, Capital								Account No. 310		
Date 20—		Explanation	Post. Ref.	Debit		Credit		Balance		
								Debit	Credit	
Apr.	1	Balance Brought Fwd.	✔						117200	00
	1		J5			18000	00		135200	00

Total Points – 6

Account Title: James Carlson, Drawing								Account No. 320		
Date		Explanation	Post. Ref.	Debit		Credit		Balance		
								Debit	Credit	

Total Points – 1

Account Title: Service Fees								Account No. 410		
Date 20—		Explanation	Post. Ref.	Debit		Credit		Balance		
								Debit	Credit	
Apr.	6		J5			9200	00		9200	00

Total Points – 4

Account Title: Advertising Expense								Account No. 510		
Date 20—		Explanation	Post. Ref.	Debit		Credit		Balance		
								Debit	Credit	
Apr.	7		J5	250	00			250	00	

Total Points – 4

Account Title: Miscellaneous Expense								Account No. 520		
Date		Explanation	Post. Ref.	Debit		Credit		Balance		
								Debit	Credit	

Total Points – 1

Account Title: *Rent Expense*   **Account No.** *530*

Date 20—		Explanation	Post. Ref.	Debit		Credit		Balance Debit		Balance Credit	
Apr.	10		J5	1200	00			1200	00		

Total Points – 4

Account Title: *Salary Expense*   **Account No.** *540*

Date 20—		Explanation	Post. Ref.	Debit		Credit		Balance Debit		Balance Credit	
Apr.	5		J5	500	00			500	00		

Total Points – 4

Account Title: *Utilities Expense*   **Account No.** *550*

Date		Explanation	Post. Ref.	Debit		Credit		Balance Debit		Balance Credit	

Total Points – 1

Teacher's Note: *Each item in this trial balance counts as* **one-half** *point, including each line of the heading, account titles, account numbers, amounts, correct totals and rulings (underlines). This problem has 56 individual items.* **Total Points – 28**

ACCOUNT TITLE	ACCT. NO.	DEBIT		CREDIT	
Carlson's Computer Service					
Trial Balance					
April 10, 20—					
Cash	110	32675	00		
Office Supplies	120	1275	00		
Office Equipment	130	18000	00		
Repair Equipment	140	6840	00		
Delivery Truck	150	7500	00		
Building	160	85000	00		
Land	170	60000	00		
Accounts Payable	210			840	00
Mortgage Payable	220			68000	00
James Carlson, Capital	310			135200	00
James Carlson, Drawing	320				
Service Fees	410			9200	00
Advertising Expense	510	250	00		
Miscellaneous Expense	520				
Rent Expense	530	1200	00		
Salary Expense	540	500	00		
Utilities Expense	550				
Totals		213240	00	213240	00

Journal	42 points
Ledger	83 points
Trial Balance	28 points
Total	153 points

VOCABULARY

Adjustments – An adjustment is an amount that is added to or subtracted from an account balance to bring the balance up to date.

Balance Sheet – A financial statement that reports assets, liabilities and owner's equity on a specific date.

Consistent Reporting – The same accounting concepts are applied the same way for each accounting period for as long as the business operates.

Fiscal Period – The length of the accounting cycle for which a business summarizes and reports financial information.

Income Statement – A financial statement that reports the revenue and expenses for a fiscal period.

Matching Expenses with Revenue – All revenue and expenses associated with a business activity are to be recorded in the same accounting period.

Net – The amount remaining after all deductions have been made.

Net Income – The difference between total revenue and total expenses when total revenue is greater than total expenses.

Net Loss – The difference between total revenue and total expenses when total expenses are greater than total revenue.

Ruling – Refers to drawing a line. A single line means the entries above are complete. A double line means the figures have been verified as correct.

Trial Balance – A proof of the equality of debits and credits in a general ledger.

Working Papers – Informal, informational papers provided by accountants to owners and managers.

Worksheet – A columnar accounting form used to summarize the general ledger information needed to prepare financial statements.

SECTION I

Worksheet for Exercise 1.1

Fox Amusement Park

Worksheet

For the Month Ended October 31, 20—

ACCT NO.	ACCOUNT NAME	TRIAL BALANCE		INCOME STATEMENT		BALANCE SHEET	
		DEBIT	CREDIT	DEBIT	CREDIT	DEBIT	CREDIT
110	Cash	4580 00				4580 00	
120	Concession Equipment	5800 00				5800 00	
130	Repair Equipment	7800 00				7800 00	
210	Concession Supply Co.		1560 00				1560 00
310	Jason Fox, Capital		10200. 00				10200 00
320	Jason Fox, Drawing	900 00				900 00	
410	Admissions Income		11500 00		11500 00		
420	Concessions Income		2600 00		2600 00		
510	Advertising Expense	2500 00		2500 00			
520	Rent Expense	3500 00		3500 00			
530	Utilities Expense	780 00		780 00			
	Totals	25860 00	25860 00	6780 00	14100 00	19080 00	11760 00
	Net Income			7320 00			7320 00
				14100 00	14100 00	19080 00	19080 00

98

Worksheet for Exercise 1.2

Johnson's Computer Service

Worksheet

For the Month Ended December 31, 20—

ACCT NO.	ACCOUNT NAME	TRIAL BALANCE DEBIT	TRIAL BALANCE CREDIT	INCOME STATEMENT DEBIT	INCOME STATEMENT CREDIT	BALANCE SHEET DEBIT	BALANCE SHEET CREDIT
110	Cash	2580 00				2580 00	
120	Computer Supplies	800 00				800 00	
130	Delivery Equipment	10600 00				10600 00	
140	Repair Equipment	7800 00				7800 00	
210	Computer Supply Co.		6560 00				6560 00
310	Kellie Johnson, Capital		19200 00				19200 00
320	Kellie Johnson, Drawing	1900 00				1900 00	
410	Computer Sales		11500 00		11500 00		
420	Repair Income		11500 00		11500 00		
510	Advertising Expense	12500 00		12500 00			
520	Miscellaneous Expense	1200 00		1200 00			
530	Rent Expense	9600 00		9600 00			
540	Utilities Expense	1780 00		1780 00			
	Totals	48760 00	48760 00	25080 00	23000 00	23680 00	25760 00
	Net Loss				2080 00	2080 00	
				25080 00	25080 00	25760 00	25760 00

Lawson's Travel Agency

Worksheet

For the Month Ended June 30, 20—

ACCT NO.	ACCOUNT NAME	TRIAL BALANCE		INCOME STATEMENT		BALANCE SHEET	
		DEBIT	CREDIT	DEBIT	CREDIT	DEBIT	CREDIT
110	Cash	9450 00				9450 00	
120	Accounts Receivable	4860 00				4860 00	
130	Office Equipment	17800 00				17800 00	
140	Office Supplies	800 00				800 00	
150	Furniture	1600 00				1600 00	
210	Accounts Payable		6890 00				6890 00
220	Sales Tax Payable		950 00				950 00
310	Donald Lawson, Capital		26390 00				26390 00
320	Donald Lawson, Drawing	900 00				900 00	
410	Fees Income		10550 00		10550 00		
510	Entertainment Expense	290 00		290 00			
520	Miscellaneous Expense	200 00		200 00			
530	Rent Expense	600 00		600 00			
540	Travel Expense	6500 00		6500 00			
550	Utilities Expense	1780 00		1780 00			
	Totals	44780 00	44780 00	9370 00	10550 00	35410 00	34230 00
	Net Income			1180 00			1180 00
				10550 00	10550 00	35410 00	35410 00

SECTION II

Worksheet for Exercise 2.1

Clever Closet Company

Worksheet

For the Month Ended October 31, 20—

ACCOUNT NAME	TRIAL BALANCE		ADJUSTMENTS		INCOME STATEMENT		BALANCE SHEET	
	DEBIT	CREDIT	DEBIT	CREDIT	DEBIT	CREDIT	DEBIT	CREDIT
Cash	13321 00						13321 00	
Petty Cash	300 00						300 00	
Supplies	3900 00			(a)1700 00			2200 00	
Prepaid Insurance	1200 00			(b) 300 00			900 00	
Tyson Office Supply		1166 00						1166 00
Office Systems, Inc.		960 00						960 00
Joanne Clever, Capital		15000 00						15000 00
Joanne Clever, Drawing	860 00						860 00	
Sales		3675 00				3675 00		
Advertising Expense	175 00				175 00			
Insurance Expense			(b) 300 00		300 00			
Miscellaneous Expense	85 00				85 00			
Rent Expense	550 00				550 00			
Repair Expense	285 00				285 00			
Supplies Expense			(a)1700 00		1700 00			
Utilities Expense	125 00				125 00			
Totals	20801 00	20801 00	2000 00	2000 00	3220 00	3675 00	17581 00	17126 00
Net Income					455 00			455 00
					3675 00	3675 00	17581 00	17581 00

SECTION III

3.1

ACCOUNT TITLE	ACCT. NO.	DEBIT		CREDIT	
		Lawrence Landscaping			
		Trial Balance			
		January 31, 20—			
Cash	*110*	*22000*	*00*		
Petty Cash	*120*	*300*	*00*		
Supplies	*130*	*2500*	*00*		
Prepaid Insurance	*140*	*1600*	*00*		
Jones Company	*210*			*5715*	*00*
Jay Lawrence, Capital	*310*			*22650*	*00*
Jay Lawrence, Drawing	*320*	*850*	*00*		
Sales	*410*			*28500*	*00*
Advertising Expense	*510*	*9950*	*00*		
Miscellaneous Expense	*520*	*165*	*00*		
Rent Expense	*530*	*12000*	*00*		
Salary Expense	*540*	*6000*	*00*		
Utility Expense	*550*	*1500*	*00*		
Totals		*56865*	*00*	*56865*	*00*

3.2

ACCOUNT TITLE	TRIAL BALANCE		INCOME STATEMENT		BALANCE SHEET	
	Debit	Credit	Debit	Credit	Debit	Credit
Cash	✔				✔	
Miscellaneous Expense	✔		✔			
Office Max		✔				✔
M. Johnson, Capital		✔				✔
Sales		✔		✔		
Office Supplies	✔				✔	
Utility Expense	✔		✔			
Insurance Expense	✔		✔			
Petty Cash	✔				✔	
Rent Expense	✔		✔			
M. Johnson, Drawing	✔				✔	
Prepaid Insurance	✔				✔	
Store Supplies	✔				✔	
Notes Payable		✔				✔

3.3

Smith's Septic Service
Worksheet
For the Month Ended November 30, 20—

ACCOUNT TITLE	ORIGINAL TRIAL BALANCE					CORRECTED TRIAL BALANCE			
	DEBIT		CREDIT			DEBIT		CREDIT	
Cash	3700	00				3700	00		
Supplies	950	00				950	00		
Prepaid Insurance	450	00				450	00		
Wooten's Chemicals			550	00				550	00
Joe's Trucking			650	00				650	00
G. Smith, Capital			3880	00				3880	00
G. Smith, Drawing	350	00				350	00		
Sales			1250	00				1250	00
Advertising Expense	305	00				350	00		
Insurance Expense									
Miscellaneous Expense	80	00				80	00		
Rent Expense	450	00				450	00		
Supplies Expense									
Totals	6285	00	6330	00		6330	00	6330	00

3.4
  a. YES   d. YES
  b. NO   e. YES
  c. YES   f. YES

Worksheet for Exercise 3.5

Floor-Shine Company
Worksheet
For the Month Ended November 30, 20—

ACCOUNT NAME	TRIAL BALANCE DEBIT	TRIAL BALANCE CREDIT	ADJUSTMENTS DEBIT	ADJUSTMENTS CREDIT	INCOME STATEMENT DEBIT	INCOME STATEMENT CREDIT	BALANCE SHEET DEBIT	BALANCE SHEET CREDIT
Cash	5844 00						5844 00	
Petty Cash	300 00						300 00	
Supplies	1900 00			(a) 600 00			1300 00	
Prepaid Insurance	800 00			(b) 400 00			400 00	
Office Systems, Inc.		60 00						60 00
Tyson Office Supply		166 00						166 00
Mike Ford, Capital		8000 00						8000 00
Mike Ford, Drawing	560 00						560 00	
Sales		1628 00				1628 00		
Advertising Expense	75 00				75 00			
Insurance Expense			(b) 400 00		400 00			
Miscellaneous Expense	15 00				15 00			
Rent Expense	250 00				250 00			
Repair Expense	85 00				85 00			
Supplies Expense			(a) 600 00		600 00			
Utilities Expense	25 00				25 00			
Totals	9854 00	9854 00	1000 00	1000 00	1450 00	1628 00	8404 00	8226 00
Net Income					178 00			178 00
					1628 00	1628 00	8404 00	8404 00

Worksheet for Exercise 3.6

Fox Photography
Worksheet
For the Quarter Ended March 31, 20—

ACCOUNT NAME	TRIAL BALANCE DEBIT	TRIAL BALANCE CREDIT	ADJUSTMENTS DEBIT	ADJUSTMENTS CREDIT	INCOME STATEMENT DEBIT	INCOME STATEMENT CREDIT	BALANCE SHEET DEBIT	BALANCE SHEET CREDIT
Cash	10454 00						10454 00	
Petty Cash	300 00						300 00	
Supplies – Office	2950 00			(a)1849 00			1101 00	
Supplies – Store	1895 00			(b)1000 00			895 00	
Prepaid Insurance	3800 00			(c)1400 00			2400 00	
Jones Office Supply		3666 00						3666 00
Maines Supply, Inc.		1660 00						1660 00
Mike Fox, Capital		12585 00						12585 00
Mike Fox, Drawing	1560 00						1560 00	
Sales		8628 00				8628 00		
Advertising Expense	2775 00				2775 00			
Insurance Expense			(c)1400 00		1400 00			
Miscellaneous Expense	615 00				615 00			
Rent Expense	1280 00				1280 00			
Repair Expense	885 00				885 00			
Supplies Expense – Office			(a)1849 00		1849 00			
Supplies Expense – Store			(b)1000 00		1000 00			
Utilities Expense	25 00				25 00			
Totals	26539 00	26539 00	4249 00	4249 00	9829 00	8628 00	16710 00	17911 00
Net Loss						1201 00	1201 00	
					9829 00	9829 00	17911 00	17911 00

Worksheet for Exercise 3.7

Bob's Boat Rental

Worksheet

For the Quarter Ended May 31, 20—

ACCOUNT NAME	TRIAL BALANCE DEBIT	TRIAL BALANCE CREDIT	ADJUSTMENTS DEBIT	ADJUSTMENTS CREDIT	INCOME STATEMENT DEBIT	INCOME STATEMENT CREDIT	BALANCE SHEET DEBIT	BALANCE SHEET CREDIT
Cash	18556 00						18556 00	
Petty Cash	450 00						450 00	
Supplies – Office	1950 00			(a) 742 00			1208 00	
Supplies – Store	2694 00			(b)1286 00			1408 00	
Prepaid Insurance	6400 00			(c) 870 00			5530 00	
Blue Heaven Marine		2981 00						2981 00
Lake View Supply, Inc.		1537 00						1537 00
Robert Borden, Capital		18688 00						18688 00
Robert Borden, Drawing	2590 00						2590 00	
Boat Rental		16548 00				16548 00		
Fishing Equipment Sales		18301 00				18301 00		
Advertising Expense	12165 00				12165 00			
Insurance Expense			(c) 870 00		870 00			
Miscellaneous Expense	2158 00				2158 00			
Rent Expense	6000 00				6000 00			
Repair Expense	2603 00				2603 00			
Supplies Expense – Office			(a) 742 00		742 00			
Supplies Expense – Store			(b)1286 00		1286 00			
Utilities Expense	2489 00				2489 00			
Totals	58055 00	58055 00	2898 00	2898 00	28313 00	34849 00	29742 00	23206 00
Net Income					6536 00			6536 00
					34849 00	34849 00	29742 00	29742 00

Worksheet for Exercise 3.8

Donald Frost, M.D.

Worksheet

For the Quarter Ended September 30, 20—

ACCOUNT NAME	TRIAL BALANCE		ADJUSTMENTS		INCOME STATEMENT		BALANCE SHEET	
	DEBIT	CREDIT	DEBIT	CREDIT	DEBIT	CREDIT	DEBIT	CREDIT
Cash	38958 00						38958 00	
Petty Cash	300 00						300 00	
Supplies – Office	4982 00			(a)3882 00			1100 00	
Supplies – Medical	5287 00			(b)2295 00			2992 00	
Prepaid Insurance	4800 00			(c)1200 00			3600 00	
Adams Office Supply		13600 00						13600 00
Johnson & Johnson, Inc.		9773 00						9773 00
Donald Frost, Capital		23514 00						23514 00
Donald Frost, Drawing	8560 00						8560 00	
Office Fees Revenue		28650 00				28650 00		
Prescription Revenue		14982 00				14982 00		
Advertising Expense	6775 00				6775 00			
Insurance Expense			(c)1200 00		1200 00			
Miscellaneous Expense	1615 00				1615 00			
Rent Expense	12450 00				12450 00			
Repair Expense	2897 00				2897 00			
Supplies Expense – Office			(a)3882 00		3882 00			
Supplies Expense – Medical			(b)2295 00		2295 00			
Utilities Expense	3895 00				3895 00			
Totals	90519 00	90519 00	7377 00	7377 00	35009 00	43632 00	55510 00	46887 00
Net Income					8623 00			8623 00
					43632 00	43632 00	55510 00	55510 00

VOCABULARY

Account Format – a balance sheet format that lists the assets on the left and the liabilities and equity on the right, similar to the accounting equation.

Balance Sheet – a financial statement that reports assets, liabilities and owner's equity on a specific date.

Fiscal Period – the length of the accounting cycle for which a business summarizes and reports financial information.

Income Statement – a financial statement that reports the revenue and expenses for a fiscal period.

Net – the amount remaining after all deductions have been made.

Net Income – the difference between total revenue and total expenses when total revenue is greater than total expenses.

Net Loss – the difference between total revenue and total expenses when total expenses are greater than total revenue.

Report Format – the most common balance sheet format, with the asset section listed first, followed by the liability and equity sections. This is a two-column report similar to the income statement.

Statement of Owner's Equity – the financial statement that reports the changes in capital that have occurred between the beginning and ending of a given fiscal period.

Worksheet – a columnar accounting form used to summarize the general ledger information needed to prepare financial statements.

SECTION I

1.1

Holiday Tours				
Income Statement				
For the Month Ended March 31, 20—				
Revenue:				
Sales	1200	00		
Membership Fees	600	00		
Total Revenue			1800	00
Expenses:				
Advertising Expense	75	00		
Miscellaneous Expense	440	00		
Rent Expense	955	00		
Utilities Expense	120	00		
Total Expenses			1590	00
Net Income			210	00

1.2

Overview Tours				
Income Statement				
For the Month Ended July 31, 20—				
Revenue:				
Sales			1200	00
Expenses:				
Advertising Expense	50	00		
Miscellaneous Expense	150	00		
Rent Expense	450	00		
Utilities Expense	40	00		
Total Expenses			690	00
Net Income			510	00

SECTION II

2.1

Bob's Boat Rental				
Statement of Owner's Equity				
For the Quarter Ended May 31, 20—				
Capital, March 1, 20—			17688	00
Add: Additional Investment	1000	00		
Net Income	6536	00		
Net Increase in Capital			7536	00
Total			25224	00
Less: Withdrawals			2590	00
Robert Borden, Capital, May 31, 20—			22634	00

2.2

Donald Frost, M.D.				
Statement of Owner's Equity				
For the Quarter Ended September 30, 20—				
Capital, July 1, 20—			23514	00
Add: Net Income			8623	00
Total			32137	00
Less: Withdrawals			8560	00
Donald Frost, Capital, September 30, 20—			23577	00

2.3

Lawson's Travel Agency					
Statement of Owner's Equity					
For the Month Ended June 30, 20—					
Capital, June 1, 20—				26390	00
Less: Net Loss	1180	00			
Withdrawals	900	00			
Net Decrease in Capital				2080	00
Rachel Lawson, Capital, June 30, 20—				24310	00

2.4

Joe Blow Duct Cleaning Service					
Statement of Owner's Equity					
For the Month Ended April 30, 20—					
Capital, April 1, 20—				15000	00
Add: Additional Investment				2500	00
Total				17500	00
Less: Net Loss	2375	00			
Withdrawals	750	00			
Net Decrease in Capital				3125	00
Joseph Blow, Capital, April 30, 20—				14375	00

SECTION III

3.1

Overview Tours				
Balance Sheet				
July 31, 20—				
Assets				
Cash	24560	00		
Petty Cash	300	00		
Office Equipment	10000	00		
Garage Equipment	900	00		
Total Assets			35760	00
Liabilities				
Staples	450	00		
Town Supply	250	00		
Total Liabilities			700	00
Owner's Equity				
John Jones, Capital			35060	00
Total Liabilities and Owner's Equity			35760	00

SECTION IV

4.1

Skate-O-Rama Company					
Income Statement					
For the Month Ended November 30, 20—					
Revenue:					
Membership Fees	6850	00			
Rental Fees	2290	00			
Total Revenue			9140	00	
Expenses:					
Advertising Expense	650	00			
Insurance Expense	910	00			
Miscellaneous Expense	475	00			
Rent Expense	1600	00			
Repair Expense	995	00			
Salary Expense	1800	00			
Supplies Expense	1285	00			
Total Expenses			7715	00	
Net Income			1425	00	

4.2 a. $985.00 net loss

b.

Smith's Garage				
Income Statement				
For the Month Ended July 31, 20—				
Revenue:				
Auto Repair Income	6122	00		
Auto Parts Income	4077	00		
Total Revenue			10199	00
Expenses:				
Advertising Expense	1812	00		
Insurance Expense	1922	00		
Miscellaneous Expense	275	00		
Rent Expense	1800	00		
Repair Expense	1095	00		
Salary Expense	2800	00		
Supplies Expense	1480	00		
Total Expenses			11184	00
Net Loss			985	00

4.3

Golf-A-Rama				
Statement of Owner's Equity				
For the Month Ended December 31, 20—				
Capital, December 1, 20—			25000	00
Add: Additional Investment	4000	00		
Net Income	7250	00		
Net Increase in Capital			11250	00
Total			36250	00
Less: Withdrawals			2600	00
Bradley Stevens, Capital, December 31, 20—			33650	00

4.4

Miller Muffin Company				
Statement of Owner's Equity				
For the Month Ended September 30, 20—				
Capital, September 1, 20—			22000	00
Add: Net Income			8500	00
Total			30500	00
Less: Withdrawals			2400	00
Melvin Miller, Capital, September 30, 20—			28100	00

4.5

Nails by Jane				
Balance Sheet				
September 30, 20—				
Assets				
Cash	2685	00		
Petty Cash	200	00		
Supplies	240	00		
Prepaid Insurance	900	00		
Total Assets			4025	00
Liabilities				
Harrison Beauty Supply	890	00		
Jones Office Supplies	240	00		
Total Liabilities			1130	00
Owner's Equity				
Jane Osgood, Capital			2895	00
Total Liabilities and Owner's Equity			4025	00

4.6

Account Title	Account Classification	Trial Balance		Financial Statements		
		Debit	Credit	Income Statement	Owner's Equity	Balance Sheet
Cash	*Asset*	✔				✔
Sales	**Revenue**		✔	✔		
Petty Cash	**Asset**	✔				✔
Members' Fees	**Revenue**		✔	✔		
Accounts Receivable	**Asset**	✔				✔
Rent Expense	**Expense**	✔		✔		
Office Supplies	**Asset**	✔				✔
Miscellaneous Expense	**Expense**	✔		✔		
Prepaid Insurance	**Asset**	✔				✔
Store Supplies	**Asset**	✔				✔
Salary Expense	**Expense**	✔		✔		
Sam's Club	**Liability**		✔			✔
Joe Wilson, Capital	**Capital**		✔		✔	✔
Commissions	**Revenue**		✔	✔		
GMAC Finance	**Liability**		✔			✔
Joe Wilson, Drawing	**Capital**	✔			✔	
Utilities Expense	**Expense**		✔	✔		

4.7

West View Garage				
Income Statement				
For the Month Ended December 31, 20—				
Revenue:				
Repair Income			5299	00
Expenses:				
Advertising Expense	1280	00		
Miscellaneous Expense	680	00		
Rent Expense	540	00		
Utilities Expense	240	00		
Total Expenses			2740	00
Net Income			2559	00

4.8

West View Garage				
Statement of Owner's Equity				
For the Month Ended December 31, 20—				
Capital, December 1, 20—			10395	00
Add: Additional Investment	2000	00		
Net Income	2559	00		
Net Increase in Capital			4559	00
Total			14954	00
Less: Withdrawals			600	00
Bruce West, Capital, December 31, 20—			14354	00

4.9

West View Garage				
Balance Sheet				
December 31, 20—				
Assets				
Cash	6284	00		
Petty Cash	400	00		
Prepaid Insurance	1115	00		
Office Supplies	250	00		
Store Supplies	775	00		
Garage Equipment	9380	00		
Total Assets			18204	00
Liabilities				
United Auto Parts	1830	00		
First City Bank	2020	00		
Total Liabilities			3850	00
Owner's Equity				
Bruce West, Capital			14354	00
Total Liabilities and Owner's Equity			18204	00

4.10

Curly-Do Salon Income Statement For the Month Ended May 31, 20—				
Revenue:				
Personal Care Income	5800	00		
Beauty Products Income	3300	00		
Total Revenue			9100	00
Expenses:				
Advertising Expense	290	00		
Insurance Expense	500	00		
Miscellaneous Expense	480	00		
Rent Expense	4800	00		
Supplies Expense – Office	1560	00		
Supplies Expense – Store	1440	00		
Utilities Expense	340	00		
Total Expenses			9410	00
Net Loss			310	00

4.11

Curly-Do Salon Statement of Owner's Equity For the Month Ended May 31, 20—				
Capital, May 1, 20—			12795	00
Less: Net Loss	310	00		
Withdrawals	1050	00		
Net Decrease in Capital			1360	00
Sue Curly, Capital, May 31, 20—			11435	00

4.12

Curly-Do Salon				
Balance Sheet				
May 31, 20—				
Assets				
Cash	6190	00		
Petty Cash	300	00		
Office Supplies	2500	00		
Store Supplies	3500	00		
Prepaid Insurance	2400	00		
Total Assets			14890	00
Liabilities				
Beauty Supply House	2890	00		
Staples Office Supply	565	00		
Total Liabilities			3455	00
Owner's Equity				
Sue Curly, Capital			11435	00
Total Liabilities and Owner's Equity			14890	00

Worksheet for Exercise 4.13

John's Fix-It Shop
Worksheet
For the Month Ended April 30, 20—

ACCOUNT NAME	TRIAL BALANCE DEBIT	TRIAL BALANCE CREDIT	ADJUSTMENTS DEBIT	ADJUSTMENTS CREDIT	INCOME STATEMENT DEBIT	INCOME STATEMENT CREDIT	BALANCE SHEET DEBIT	BALANCE SHEET CREDIT
Cash	3750 00						3750 00	
Petty Cash	100 00						100 00	
Supplies – Office	1800 00			(a) 890 00			910 00	
Supplies – Parts	1600 00			(b) 805 00			795 00	
Prepaid Insurance	950 00			(c) 200 00			750 00	
Equipment	3775 00						3775 00	
Johnson Supply		375 00						375 00
Wells Company		900 00						900 00
John Goodie, Capital		7875 00						7875 00
John Goodie, Drawing	430 00						430 00	
Parts Sales		1975 00				1975 00		
Repair Sales		2850 00				2850 00		
Advertising Expense	470 00				470 00			
Insurance Expense			(c) 200 00		200 00			
Miscellaneous Expense	130 00				130 00			
Rent Expense	600 00				600 00			
Supplies Expense – Office			(a) 890 00		890 00			
Supplies Expense – Parts			(b) 805 00		805 00			
Utilities Expense	370 00				370 00			
Totals	13975 00	13975 00	1895 00	1895 00	3465 00	4825 00	10510 00	9150 00
Net Income					1360 00			1360 00
					4825 00	4825 00	10510 00	10510 00

4.14

John's Fix-It Shop				
Income Statement				
For the Month Ended April 30, 20—				
Revenue:				
Parts Sales	1975	00		
Repair Sales	2850	00		
Total Revenue			4825	00
Expenses:				
Advertising Expense	470	00		
Insurance Expense	200	00		
Miscellaneous Expense	130	00		
Rent Expense	600	00		
Supplies Expense – Office	890	00		
Supplies Expense – Parts	805	00		
Utilities Expense	370	00		
Total Expenses			3465	00
Net Income			1360	00

4.15

John's Fix-It Shop				
Statement of Owner's Equity				
For the Month Ended April 30, 20—				
Capital, April 1, 20—			7875	00
Add: Net Income			1360	00
Total			9235	00
Less: Withdrawals			430	00
John Goodie, Capital, April 30, 20—			8805	00

4.16

John's Fix-It Shop					
Balance Sheet					
April 30, 20—					
Assets					
Cash	3750	00			
Petty Cash	100	00			
Supplies – Office	910	00			
Supplies – Parts	795	00			
Prepaid Insurance	750	00			
Equipment	3775	00			
Total Assets			10080	00	
Liabilities					
Johnson Supply	375	00			
Wells Company	900	00			
Total Liabilities			1275	00	
Owner's Equity					
John Goodie, Capital			8805	00	
Total Liabilities and Owner's Equity			10080	00	

VOCABULARY

Adjusting Entries – entries made in the journal to adjust the ledger accounts so that they will contain the same balances as shown on the worksheet.

Adjustment – an amount that is added to or subtracted from an account balance to bring the balance up to date.

Assets/Expense Adjustment – a type of deferral adjustment that distributes the expense of consumed assets (such as supplies) over more than one fiscal period.

Balance Sheet – a financial statement that reports assets, liabilities and owner's equity on a specific date.

Closing Entries – journal entries prepared at the end of a fiscal period to transfer the balances of revenue and expense accounts to the proprietor's Capital account.

Consistent Reporting – the same accounting concepts are applied the same way for each accounting period for as long as the business operates.

Deferral Adjustments – adjustments to accounts that delay the recognition of the expenses or revenue until a fiscal period later than the one during which the cash was paid or the liability incurred.

Fiscal Period – the length of the accounting cycle for which a business summarizes and reports financial information.

Income Statement – a financial statement that reports the revenue and expenses for a fiscal period.

Income Summary Account – a temporary account whose balance is transferred to the permanent Capital account at the end of each accounting period.

Matching Expenses with Revenue – all revenue and expenses associated with a business activity are to be recorded in the same accounting period.

Net Income – the difference between total revenue and total expenses when total revenue is greater than total expenses.

Net Loss – the difference between total revenue and total expenses when total expenses are greater than total revenue.

Permanent Accounts – accounts that accumulate financial information from one fiscal period to another; also known as real accounts.

Post-Closing Trial Balance – a trial balance completed to check the equality of the debits and credits in the general ledger accounts that remain open after the closing process has been completed.

Temporary Accounts – accounts that accumulate financial information until it is transferred to the owner's Capital account; also known as nominal accounts.

Trial Balance – a proof of the equality of debits and credits in a general ledger.

Working Papers – informal papers in the form of memoranda, analysis papers, and informal reports.

Worksheet – a columnar accounting form used to summarize the general ledger information needed to prepare financial statements.

SECTION I

1.1

JOURNAL								Page 2	
Date 20—		Account Title and Explanation	Doc No.	Post. Ref.	General Debit			General Credit	
		Adjusting Entries							
July	31	Supplies Expense		550	1341	00			
		Supplies		130				1341	00
	31	Insurance Expense		520	330	00			
		Prepaid Insurance		140				330	00

Account Title: Supplies   **Account No.** 130

Date 20—		Explanation	Post. Ref.	Debit		Credit		Balance			
								Debit		Credit	
July	1		✔					4319	00		
	31		J2			1341	00	2978	00		

Account Title: Prepaid Insurance   **Account No.** 140

Date 20—		Explanation	Post. Ref.	Debit		Credit		Balance			
								Debit		Credit	
July	1		✔					1600	00		
	31		J2			330	00	1270	00		

Account Title: Insurance Expense   **Account No.** 520

Date 20—		Explanation	Post. Ref.	Debit		Credit		Balance			
								Debit		Credit	
July	31		J2	330	00			330	00		

Account Title: Supplies Expense   **Account No.** 550

Date 20—		Explanation	Post. Ref.	Debit		Credit		Balance			
								Debit		Credit	
July	31		J2	1341	00			1341	00		

SECTION II

2.1 **Teacher's Note:** Make sure the student has entered the posting reference numbers in the journal on page 20 (shown below).

JOURNAL						Page 2	
Date 20—		Account Title and Explanation	Doc No.	Post. Ref.	General Debit		General Credit
		Adjusting Entries					
Apr.	30	*Supplies Expense*		560	1849 00		
		Supplies		130			1849 00
	30	*Insurance Expense*		520	1400 00		
		Prepaid Insurance		140			1400 00
		Closing Entries					
	30	*Sales*		410	8834 00		
		Income Summary		330			8834 00
1	30	*Income Summary* 2		**330**	11 7549 00		
		3 *Advertising Expense*		**510**			4 1775 00
		5 *Insurance Expense*		**520**			1400 00
		6 *Miscellaneous Expense*		**530**			615 00
		7 *Rent Expense*		**540**			1000 00
		8 *Repair Expense*		**550**			885 00
		9 *Supplies Expense*		**560**			1849 00
		10 *Utilities Expense*		**570**			25 00

Account Title: *Income Summary*					Account No. 330			
Date 20—		Explanation	Post. Ref.	Debit	Credit	Balance		
						Debit	Credit	
Apr.	30		J2		8834 00		8834 00	
	30		J2	7549 00			1285 00	

Account Title: *Sales*					Account No. 410			
Date 20—		Explanation	Post. Ref.	Debit	Credit	Balance		
						Debit	Credit	
Apr.	15		J1		4450 00		4450 00	
	22		J1		4384 00		8834 00	
	30		J2	8834 00				

Account Title: *Advertising Expense* — **Account No.** 510

Date 20—		Explanation	Post. Ref.	Debit		Credit		Balance			
								Debit		Credit	
Apr.	3		J1	750	00			750	00		
	16		J1	1025	00			1775	00		
	30		J2			1775	00	—			

Account Title: *Insurance Expense* — **Account No.** 520

Date 20—		Explanation	Post. Ref.	Debit		Credit		Balance			
								Debit		Credit	
Apr.	30		J2	1400	00			1400	00		
	30		J2			1400	00	—			

Account Title: *Miscellaneous Expense* — **Account No.** 530

Date 20—		Explanation	Post. Ref.	Debit		Credit		Balance			
								Debit		Credit	
Apr.	15		J1	615	00			615	00		
	30		J2			615	00	—			

Account Title: *Rent Expense* — **Account No.** 540

Date 20—		Explanation	Post. Ref.	Debit		Credit		Balance			
								Debit		Credit	
Apr.	1		J1	1000	00			1000	00		
	30		J2			1000	00	—			

Account Title: *Repair Expense* — **Account No.** 550

Date 20—		Explanation	Post. Ref.	Debit		Credit		Balance			
								Debit		Credit	
Apr.	7		J1	800	00			800	00		
	24		J1	85	00			885	00		
	30		J2			885	00	—			

Account Title: Supplies Expense   Account No. 560

Date 20—		Explanation	Post. Ref.	Debit		Credit		Balance			
								Debit		Credit	
Apr.	30		J2	1849	00			1849	00		
	30		J2			1849	00	——	——		

Account Title: Utilities Expense   Account No. 570

Date 20—		Explanation	Post. Ref.	Debit		Credit		Balance			
								Debit		Credit	
Apr.	12		J1	25	00			25	00		
	30		J2			25	00	——	——		

2.2

JOURNAL							Page 5	
Date 20—		Account Title and Explanation	Doc No.	Post. Ref.	General Debit		General Credit	
		Adjusting Entries						
Mar.	31	Supplies Expense			2849	00		
		Supplies					2849	00
	31	Insurance Expense			1400	00		
		Prepaid Insurance					1400	00
		Closing Entries						
	31	Sales			8628	00		
		Income Summary					8628	00
	31	Income Summary			9829	00		
		Advertising Expense					2775	00
		Insurance Expense					1400	00
		Miscellaneous Expense					615	00
		Rent Expense					1280	00
		Repair Expense					885	00
		Supplies Expense					2849	00
		Utilities Expense					25	00
	31	Mike Fox, Capital			1201	00		
		Income Summary					1201	00
	31	Mike Fox, Capital			1560	00		
		Mike Fox, Drawing					1560	00

SECTION III

3.1

ACCOUNT TITLE	ACCT. NO.	DEBIT		CREDIT	
Clever Closet Company					
Post-Closing Trial Balance					
May 31, 20—					
Cash	110	13321	00		
Petty Cash	120	300	00		
Supplies	130	2200	00		
Prepaid Insurance	140	900	00		
Tyson Office Supply	210			1166	00
Office Systems, Inc.	220			960	00
Joanne Clever, Capital	310			14595	00
Totals		16721	00	16721	00

SECTION IV

4.1

JOURNAL								Page 3	
Date 20—		Account Title and Explanation	Doc No.	Post. Ref.	General Debit		General Credit		
		Adjusting Entries							
July	31	*Supplies Expense – Office*		530	600	00			
		Supplies – Office		130			600	00	
	31	*Supplies Expense – Store*		540	850	00			
		Supplies – Store		140			850	00	
	31	*Insurance Expense*		520	900	00			
		Prepaid Insurance		150			900	00	

4.2

Account Title: Supplies – Office   Account No. 130

Date 20—		Explanation	Post. Ref.	Debit		Credit		Balance Debit		Balance Credit	
July	1		✔					800	00		
	10		J1	400	00			1200	00		
	21		J2	450	00			1650	00		
	31		J3			600	00	1050	00		

Account Title: Supplies – Store   Account No. 140

Date 20—		Explanation	Post. Ref.	Debit		Credit		Balance Debit		Balance Credit	
July	1		✔					1850	00		
	15		J1	250	00			2100	00		
	25		J2	680	00			2780	00		
	31		J3			850	00	1930	00		

Account Title: *Prepaid Insurance*					Account No. *150*		
Date 20—	Explanation	Post. Ref.	Debit	Credit	Balance		
					Debit	Credit
July 1		✔			800 00	
15		J2	1200 00		2000 00	
31		J3		900 00	1100 00	

Account Title: *Insurance Expense*					Account No. *520*		
Date 20—	Explanation	Post. Ref.	Debit	Credit	Balance		
					Debit	Credit
July 31		J3	900 00		900 00	

Account Title: *Supplies Expense – Office*					Account No. *530*		
Date 20—	Explanation	Post. Ref.	Debit	Credit	Balance		
					Debit	Credit
July 31		J3	600 00		600 00	

Account Title: *Supplies Expense – Store*					Account No. *540*		
Date 20—	Explanation	Post. Ref.	Debit	Credit	Balance		
					Debit	Credit
July 31		J3	850 00		850 00	

4.3

JOURNAL								Page *3*
Date 20—		Account Title and Explanation	Doc No.	Post. Ref.	General Debit		General Credit	
		Closing Entries						
July	31	Sales		410	11160	00		
		Income Summary		330			11160	00
	31	Income Summary		330	8270	00		
		Advertising Expense		510			3450	00
		Credit Card Fee Expense		520			260	00
		Insurance Expense		530			220	00
		Miscellaneous Expense		540			380	00
		Rent Expense		550			1200	00
		Salary Expense		560			1900	00
		Supplies Expense – Office		570			480	00
		Supplies Expense – Store		580			380	00
	31	Income Summary		330	2890	00		
		John Harrison, Capital		310			2890	00
	31	John Harrison, Capital		310	1200	00		
		John Harrison, Drawing		320			1200	00

4.4

Account Title: *John Harrison, Capital* **Account No.** 310

Date 20—		Explanation	Post. Ref.	Debit		Credit		Balance			
								Debit		Credit	
July	1		✔							10960	00
	31		J3			2890	00			13850	00
	31		J3	1200	00					12650	00

Account Title: *John Harrison, Drawing* **Account No.** 320

Date 20—		Explanation	Post. Ref.	Debit		Credit		Balance			
								Debit		Credit	
July	15		J1	600	00			600	00		
	30		J1	600	00			1200	00		
	31		J3			1200	00	—			

Account Title: *Income Summary* **Account No.** 330

Date 20—		Explanation	Post. Ref.	Debit		Credit		Balance			
								Debit		Credit	
July	31		J3			11160	00			11160	00
	31		J3	8270	00					2890	00
	31		J3	2890	00					—	

Account Title: *Sales* **Account No.** 410

Date 20—		Explanation	Post. Ref.	Debit		Credit		Balance			
								Debit		Credit	
July	7		J1			2790	00			2790	00
	14		J1			2000	00			4790	00
	21		J2			2370	00			7160	00
	30		J2			4000	00			11160	00
	31		J3	11160	00					—	

Account Title: Advertising Expense — **Account No.** 510

Date 20—		Explanation	Post. Ref.	Debit		Credit		Balance Debit		Balance Credit	
July	5		J1	1450	00			1450	00		
	15		J1	1200	00			2650	00		
	20		J2	800	00			3450	00		
	31		J3			3450	00	——			

Account Title: Credit Card Fee Expense — **Account No.** 520

Date 20—		Explanation	Post. Ref.	Debit		Credit		Balance Debit		Balance Credit	
July	25		J2	260	00			260	00		
	31		J3			260	00	——			

Account Title: Insurance Expense — **Account No.** 530

Date 20—		Explanation	Post. Ref.	Debit		Credit		Balance Debit		Balance Credit	
July	31		J2	220	00			220	00		
	31		J3			220	00	——			

Account Title: Miscellaneous Expense — **Account No.** 540

Date 20—		Explanation	Post. Ref.	Debit		Credit		Balance Debit		Balance Credit	
July	6		J1	180	00			180	00		
	10		J1	200	00			380	00		
	31		J3			380	00	——			

Account Title: Rent Expense — **Account No.** 550

Date 20—		Explanation	Post. Ref.	Debit		Credit		Balance Debit		Balance Credit	
July	1		J1	1200	00			1200	00		
	31		J3			1200	00	——			

Account Title: *Salary Expense*						Account No. *560*			
Date 20—		Explanation	Post. Ref.	Debit		Credit		Balance	
								Debit	Credit
July	14		J1	950	00			950	00		
	28		J2	950	00			1900	00		
	31		J3			1900	00	——			

Account Title: *Supplies Expense – Office*						Account No. *570*			
Date 20—		Explanation	Post. Ref.	Debit		Credit		Balance	
								Debit	Credit
July	31		J3	480	00			480	00		
	31		J3			480	00	——			

Account Title: *Supplies Expense – Store*						Account No. *580*			
Date 20—		Explanation	Post. Ref.	Debit		Credit		Balance	
								Debit	Credit
July	31		J3	380	00			380	00		
	31		J3			380	00	——			

4.5

Date 20—		Account Title and Explanation	Doc No.	Post. Ref.	General Debit		General Credit	
		JOURNAL					Page 2	
		Closing Entries						
Sept.	30	Commissions			5200	00		
		Income Summary					5200	00
	30	Income Summary			4410	00		
		Advertising Expense					290	00
		Insurance Expense					500	00
		Miscellaneous Expense					480	00
		Rent Expense					1800	00
		Supplies Expense – Office					560	00
		Supplies Expense – Store					440	00
		Utilities Expense					340	00
	30	Income Summary			790	00		
		Rufus Hartman, Capital					790	00
	30	Rufus Hartman, Capital			950	00		
		Rufus Hartman, Drawing					950	00

Account Title: Cash — Account No. 110

Date 20—		Explanation	Post. Ref.	Debit		Credit		Balance Debit		Balance Credit	
Nov.	30		✔					3600	00		

Account Title: Petty Cash — Account No. 120

Date 20—		Explanation	Post. Ref.	Debit		Credit		Balance Debit		Balance Credit	
Nov.	30		✔					300	00		

Account Title: *Office Supplies* — **Account No.** 130

Date 20—		Explanation	Post. Ref.	Debit		Credit		Balance Debit		Balance Credit	
Nov.	30		✔					950	00		
	30		J4			500	00	450	00		

Account Title: *Store Supplies* — **Account No.** 140

Date 20—		Explanation	Post. Ref.	Debit		Credit		Balance Debit		Balance Credit	
Nov.	30		✔					850	00		
	30		J4			600	00	250	00		

Account Title: *Prepaid Insurance* — **Account No.** 150

Date 20—		Explanation	Post. Ref.	Debit		Credit		Balance Debit		Balance Credit	
Nov.	30		✔					540	00		
	30		J4			200	00	340	00		

Account Title: *Equipment* — **Account No.** 160

Date 20—		Explanation	Post. Ref.	Debit		Credit		Balance Debit		Balance Credit	
Nov.	30		✔					7595	00		

Account Title: *Bern Company* — **Account No.** 210

Date 20—		Explanation	Post. Ref.	Debit		Credit		Balance Debit		Balance Credit	
Nov.	30		✔							500	00

Account Title: *Kelly Company* **Account No.** 220

Date 20—		Explanation	Post. Ref.	Debit		Credit		Balance			
								Debit		Credit	
Nov.	30		✔							120	00

Account Title: *Donna Howard, Capital* **Account No.** 310

Date 20—		Explanation	Post. Ref.	Debit		Credit		Balance			
								Debit		Credit	
Nov.	30		✔							12765	00
	30		J4	300	00					12465	00
	30		J4	550	00					11915	00

Account Title: *Donna Howard, Drawing* **Account No.** 320

Date 20—		Explanation	Post. Ref.	Debit		Credit		Balance			
								Debit		Credit	
Nov.	30		✔	550	00			550	00		
	30		J4			550	00	—			

Account Title: *Income Summary* **Account No.** 330

Date 20—		Explanation	Post. Ref.	Debit		Credit		Balance			
								Debit		Credit	
Nov.	30		J4			2300	00			2300	00
	30		J4	2600	00			300	00		
	30		J4			300	00	—			

Account Title: *Sales* **Account No.** 410

Date 20—		Explanation	Post. Ref.	Debit		Credit		Balance			
								Debit		Credit	
Nov.	30		✔							2300	00
	30		J4	2300	00			—			

Account Title: *Advertising Expense*   **Account No.** *510*

Date 20—		Explanation	Post. Ref.	Debit		Credit		Balance Debit		Balance Credit	
Nov.	30		✔					600	00		
	30		J4			600	00	——			

Account Title: *Insurance Expense*   **Account No.** *520*

Date 20—		Explanation	Post. Ref.	Debit		Credit		Balance Debit		Balance Credit	
Nov.	30		J4	200	00			200	00		
	30		J4			200	00	——			

Account Title: *Miscellaneous Expense*   **Account No.** *530*

Date 20—		Explanation	Post. Ref.	Debit		Credit		Balance Debit		Balance Credit	
Nov.	30		✔					185	00		
	30		J4			185	00	——			

Account Title: *Rent Expense*   **Account No.** *540*

Date 20—		Explanation	Post. Ref.	Debit		Credit		Balance Debit		Balance Credit	
Nov.	30		✔					425	00		
	30		J4			425	00	——			

Account Title: *Repair Expense*   **Account No.** *550*

Date 20—		Explanation	Post. Ref.	Debit		Credit		Balance Debit		Balance Credit	
Nov.	30		✔					90	00		
	30		J4			90	00	——			

Account Title: *Supplies Expense – Office*								Account No. *560*			
Date 20–		**Explanation**	**Post. Ref.**	**Debit**		**Credit**		**Balance**			
								Debit		**Credit**	
Nov.	30		J4	500	00			500	00		
	30		J4			500	00				

Account Title: *Supplies Expense – Store*								Account No. *570*			
Date 20–		**Explanation**	**Post. Ref.**	**Debit**		**Credit**		**Balance**			
								Debit		**Credit**	
Nov.	30		J4	600	00			600	00		
	30		J4			600	00				

Worksheet for Exercise 4.6

Howard's Florist

Worksheet

For the Month Ended November 30, 20—

ACCOUNT NAME	TRIAL BALANCE		ADJUSTMENTS		INCOME STATEMENT		BALANCE SHEET	
	DEBIT	CREDIT	DEBIT	CREDIT	DEBIT	CREDIT	DEBIT	CREDIT
Cash	3600 00						3600 00	
Petty Cash	300 00						300 00	
Office Supplies	950 00			(a) 500 00			450 00	
Store Supplies	850 00			(b) 600 00			250 00	
Prepaid Insurance	540 00			(c) 200 00			340 00	
Equipment	7595 00						7595 00	
Bern Company		500 00						500 00
Kelly Company		120 00						120 00
Donna Howard, Capital		12765 00						12765 00
Donna Howard, Drawing	550 00						550 00	
Sales		2300 00				2300 00		
Advertising Expense	600 00				600 00			
Insurance Expense			(c) 200 00		200 00			
Miscellaneous Expense	185 00				185 00			
Rent Expense	425 00				425 00			
Repair Expense	90 00				90 00			
Supplies Expense – Office			(a) 500 00		500 00			
Supplies Expense – Store			(b) 600 00		600 00			
Totals	15685 00	15685 00	1300 00	1300 00	2600 00	2300 00	13085 00	13385 00
Net Loss						300 00	300 00	
					2600 00	2600 00	13385 00	13385 00

4.7–4.8

			JOURNAL			Page *4*	

Date 20—		Account Title and Explanation	Doc No.	Post. Ref.	General Debit		General Credit	
		Adjusting Entries						
Nov.	30	*Supplies Expense – Office*		560	500	00		
		Office Supplies		130			500	00
	30	*Supplies Expense – Store*		570	600	00		
		Store Supplies		140			600	00
	30	*Insurance Expense*		520	200	00		
		Prepaid Insurance		150			200	00
		Closing Entries						
	30	*Sales*		410	2300	00		
		Income Summary		330			2300	00
	30	*Income Summary*		330	2600	00		
		Advertising Expense		510			600	00
		Insurance Expense		520			200	00
		Miscellaneous Expense		530			185	00
		Rent Expense		540			425	00
		Repair Expense		550			90	00
		Supplies Expense – Office		560			500	00
		Supplies Expense – Store		570			600	00
	30	*Donna Howard, Capital*		310	300	00		
		Income Summary		330			300	00
	30	*Donna Howard, Capital*		310	550	00		
		Donna Howard, Drawing		320			550	00

4.9

Howard's Florist					
Post-Closing Trial Balance					
November 30, 20—					
ACCOUNT TITLE	ACCT. NO.	DEBIT		CREDIT	
Cash	110	3600	00		
Petty Cash	120	300	00		
Office Supplies	130	450	00		
Store Supplies	140	250	00		
Prepaid Insurance	150	340	00		
Equipment	160	7595	00		
Bern Company	210			500	00
Kelly Company	220			120	00
Donna Howard, Capital	310			11915	00
Totals		12535	00	12535	00

OPTIONAL EXERCISES FOR EXTRA CREDIT

Teacher's Note: *Items in* **bolded italics** *are answers to be graded. Answers count* **one-half** *point each.*

Account Title: *Cash*   **Account No.** *110*

Date 20—		Explanation	Post. Ref.	Debit		Credit		Balance			
								Debit		Credit	
Dec.	31		✔					1550	00		

Account Title: *Petty Cash*   **Account No.** *120*

Date 20—		Explanation	Post. Ref.	Debit		Credit		Balance			
								Debit		Credit	
Dec.	31		✔					200	00		

Account Title: *Office Supplies*   **Account No.** *130*

Date 20—		Explanation	Post. Ref.	Debit		Credit		Balance			
								Debit		Credit	
Dec.	31		✔					1280	00		
	31		*J3*			*365*	*00*	*915*	*00*		

Account Title: *Prepaid Insurance*   **Account No.** *140*

Date 20—		Explanation	Post. Ref.	Debit		Credit		Balance			
								Debit		Credit	
Dec.	31		✔					2400	00		
	31		*J3*			*360*	*00*	*2040*	*00*		

Account Title: *Law Library*   **Account No.** *150*

Date 20—		Explanation	Post. Ref.	Debit		Credit		Balance			
								Debit		Credit	
Dec.	31		✔					2500	00		

Account Title: *Equipment* **Account No.** *160*

Date 20—		Explanation	Post. Ref.	Debit		Credit		Balance Debit		Credit	
Dec.	31		✔					5600	00		

Account Title: *Computer Services* **Account No.** *210*

Date 20—		Explanation	Post. Ref.	Debit		Credit		Balance Debit		Credit	
Dec.	31		✔							760	00

Account Title: *Fox's Office Supply* **Account No.** *220*

Date 20—		Explanation	Post. Ref.	Debit		Credit		Balance Debit		Credit	
Dec.	31		✔							415	00

Account Title: *Prentice-Hall* **Account No.** *230*

Date 20—		Explanation	Post. Ref.	Debit		Credit		Balance Debit		Credit	
Dec.	31		✔							1840	00

Account Title: *Keri Downs, Capital* **Account No.** *310*

Date 20—		Explanation	Post. Ref.	Debit		Credit		Balance Debit		Credit	
Dec.	31		✔							9200	00
	31		J3			1690	00			10890	00
	31		J3	1100	00					9790	00

Account Title: *Keri Downs, Drawing*   **Account No.** *320*

Date 20—		Explanation	Post. Ref.	Debit		Credit		Balance Debit		Credit	
Dec.	31		✔					1100	00		
	31		J3			1100	00	——			

Account Title: *Income Summary*   **Account No.** *330*

Date 20—		Explanation	Post. Ref.	Debit		Credit		Balance Debit		Credit	
Dec.	31		J3			5250	00			5250	00
	31		J3	3560	00					1690	00
	31		J3	1690	00					——	

Account Title: *Legal Fees Income*   **Account No.** *410*

Date 20—		Explanation	Post. Ref.	Debit		Credit		Balance Debit		Credit	
Dec.	31		✔							5250	00
	31		J3			5250	00			——	

Account Title: *Advertising Expense*   **Account No.** *510*

Date 20—		Explanation	Post. Ref.	Debit		Credit		Balance Debit		Credit	
Dec.	31		✔					125	00		
	31		J3			125	00	——			

Account Title: *Insurance Expense*   **Account No.** *520*

Date 20—		Explanation	Post. Ref.	Debit		Credit		Balance Debit		Credit	
Dec.	31		J3	360	00			360	00		
	31		J3			360	00	——			

Account Title: *Miscellaneous Expense*   **Account No.** 530

Date 20—		Explanation	Post. Ref.	Debit		Credit		Balance Debit		Balance Credit	
Dec.	31		✔					80	00		
	31		J3			80	00	——			

Account Title: *Rent Expense*   **Account No.** 540

Date 20—		Explanation	Post. Ref.	Debit		Credit		Balance Debit		Balance Credit	
Dec.	1		✔					1000	00		
	31		J3			1000	00	——			

Account Title: *Salary Expense*   **Account No.** 550

Date 20—		Explanation	Post. Ref.	Debit		Credit		Balance Debit		Balance Credit	
Dec.	31		✔					1400	00		
	31		J3			1400	00	——			

Account Title: *Supplies Expense – Office*   **Account No.** 560

Date 20—		Explanation	Post. Ref.	Debit		Credit		Balance Debit		Balance Credit	
Dec.	31		J3	365	00			365	00		
	31		J3			365	00	——			

Account Title: *Utilities Expense*   **Account No.** 570

Date 20—		Explanation	Post. Ref.	Debit		Credit		Balance Debit		Balance Credit	
Dec.	1		✔					230	00		
	31		J3			230	00	——			

Keri Downs, Attorney

Worksheet

For the Month Ended December 31, 20—

ACCOUNT NAME	TRIAL BALANCE DEBIT	TRIAL BALANCE CREDIT	ADJUSTMENTS DEBIT	ADJUSTMENTS CREDIT	INCOME STATEMENT DEBIT	INCOME STATEMENT CREDIT	BALANCE SHEET DEBIT	BALANCE SHEET CREDIT
Cash	1550 00						1550 00	
Petty Cash	200 00						200 00	
Office Supplies	1280 00			(a) 365 00			915 00	
Prepaid Insurance	2400 00			(b) 360 00			2040 00	
Law Library	2500 00						2500 00	
Equipment	5600 00						5600 00	
Computer Services		760 00						760 00
Fox's Office Supply		415 00						415 00
Prentice-Hall		1840 00						1840 00
Keri Downs, Capital		9200 00						9200 00
Keri Downs, Drawing	1100 00						1100 00	
Legal Fees Income		5250 00				5250 00		
Advertising Expense	125 00				125 00			
Insurance Expense			(b) 360 00		360 00			
Miscellaneous Expense	80 00				80 00			
Rent Expense	1000 00				1000 00			
Salary Expense	1400 00				1400 00			
Supplies Expense – Office			(a) 365 00		365 00			
Utilities Expense	230 00				230 00			
Totals	17465 00	17465 00	725 00	725 00	3560 00	5250 00	13905 00	12215 00
Net Income					1690 00			1690 00
					5250 00	5250 00	13905 00	13905 00

Income Statement:

Keri Downs, Attorney					
Income Statement					
For the Month Ended December 31, 20—					
Revenue:					
Legal Fees Income				5250	00
Expenses:					
Advertising Expense	125	00			
Insurance Expense	360	00			
Miscellaneous Expense	80	00			
Rent Expense	1000	00			
Salary Expense	1400	00			
Supplies Expense – Office	365	00			
Utilities Expense	230	00			
Total Expenses				3560	00
Net Income				1690	00

Statement of Owner's Equity:

Keri Downs, Attorney					
Statement of Owner's Equity					
For the Month Ended December 31, 20—					
Capital, December 1, 20—				9200	00
Add: Net Income				1690	00
Total				10890	00
Less: Withdrawals				1100	00
Keri Downs, Capital, December 31, 20—				9790	00

Balance Sheet:

Keri Downs, Attorney				
Balance Sheet				
December 31, 20—				
Assets				
Cash	1550	00		
Petty Cash	200	00		
Office Supplies	915	00		
Prepaid Insurance	2040	00		
Law Library	2500	00		
Equipment	5600	00		
Total Assets			12805	00
Liabilities				
Computer Services	760	00		
Fox's Office Supply	415	00		
Prentice-Hall	1840	00		
Total Liabilities			3015	00
Owner's Equity				
Keri Downs, Capital			9790	00
Total Liabilities and Owner's Equity			12805	00

Journal:

JOURNAL					General Debit		General Credit		Page 3	
Date 20—		Account Title and Explanation	Doc No.	Post. Ref.						
		Adjusting Entries								
Dec.	31	Supplies Expense – Office		560	365	00				
		Office Supplies		130			365	00		
	31	Insurance Expense		520	360	00				
		Prepaid Insurance		140			360	00		
		Closing Entries								
	31	Legal Fees Income		410	5250	00				
		Income Summary		330			5250	00		
	31	Income Summary		330	3560	00				
		Advertising Expense		510			125	00		
		Insurance Expense		520			360	00		
		Miscellaneous Expense		530			80	00		
		Rent Expense		540			1000	00		
		Salary Expense		550			1400	00		
		Supplies Expense – Office		560			365	00		
		Utilities Expense		570			230	00		
	31	Income Summary		330	1690	00				
		Keri Downs, Capital		310			1690	00		
	31	Keri Downs, Capital		310	1100	00				
		Keri Downs, Drawing		320			1100	00		

Post-Closing Trial Balance:

ACCOUNT TITLE	ACCT. NO.	DEBIT		CREDIT	
Keri Downs, Attorney					
Post-Closing Trial Balance					
December 31, 20—					
Cash	110	1550	00		
Petty Cash	120	200	00		
Office Supplies	130	915	00		
Prepaid Insurance	140	2040	00		
Law Library	150	2500	00		
Equipment	160	5600	00		
Computer Services	210			760	00
Fox's Office Supply	220			415	00
Prentice-Hall	230			1840	00
Keri Downs, Capital	310			9790	00
Totals		12805	00	12805	00

Ledger	37.5 points
Worksheet	41.0 points
Income Statement	14.0 points
Statement of Owner's Equity	8.0 points
Balance Sheet	19.0 points
Journal	32.5 points
Post-Closing Trial Balance	19.0 points
Total Points	**171.0 points**

VOCABULARY

Employee Earnings Record – a form used to summarize payroll payments made to each individual employee.

Federal Unemployment Tax (FUTA) – a federal tax used for administration of state and federal unemployment programs.

Federal Insurance Contribution Act (FICA) – a law requiring employers and employees to pay taxes to the federal government to support the Social Security programs; "FICA" also refers to the taxes themselves.

Gross Earnings – the total amount due each employee for the pay period before any payroll deductions; also referred to as gross pay.

Pay Period – a period covered by a salary payment.

Payroll – all salaries and wages paid to employees.

Payroll Deductions – required and voluntary deductions from gross earnings to determine net pay.

Payroll Register – an accounting form that summarizes payroll information for all employees during a specific pay period.

Quarterly – every three months; in a calendar year the quarters are January through March, April through June, July through September and October through December.

Salary – a payment plan that pays employees a fixed amount for each pay period.

Semimonthly – twice a month; refers to a pay period that usually falls on the 15th·and the 31st the month.

State Unemployment Tax – a tax imposed by a state to pay benefits to the unemployed.

Time and a Half – a term used to describe the rate a worker is paid for overtime. The overtime rate is the worker's regular hourly rate ("time") plus half his regular rate ("and a half").

Wages – payment based on an hourly rate or a piecework basis.

Withholding Allowance – the number of persons legally supported by the taxpayer.

SECTION I (see Self Test 1)

SECTION II

2.1   a. $408.00

      b. $270.00

      c. $418.00

      d. $624.00

2.2   a. $12.00 x 1.5 $18.00

      b. $6.75 x 1.5 $10.125

      c. $11.00 x 1.5 $16.50

      d. $16.00 x 1.5 $24.00

2.3   a. 2

      b. 8

      c. 13

      d. 0

      e. 6

2.4   **Employee #1:**

	Regular Hours	Overtime Hours
a.	8	2
b.	6	0
c.	8	1
d.	7	0
e.	8	3
f.	37	6

Employee #2:

	Regular Hours	Overtime Hours
a.	8	1
b.	8	0
c.	8	2
d.	5	0
e.	8	4
f.	37	7

2.5   a. $157.50

      b. $453.60

      c. $204.38

      d. $316.25

      e. $318.16

      f. $299.00

2.6

	Payroll Time In	Payroll Time Out
a.	8:00	12:00
b.	12:00	1:00
c.	9:00	1:00
d.	8:00	12:30
e.	7:45	11:00

2.7

Employee	Sue Wetzel
Employee #	13
Period Ending	December 31, 20—

ABC Company

DATE	MORNING		AFTERNOON		OVERTIME		HOURS	
	IN	OUT	IN	OUT	IN	OUT	REG	OT
12/27	7:59	12:02	12:55	5:06			8	0
12/28	8:01	12:00	12:55	5:01	6:03	8:57	8	3
12/29	8:00	12:00	12:59	5:00			8	0
12/30	7:56	11:58	1:01	5:04			8	0
12/31	7:55	12:03	12:58	5:02	6:30	9:06	8	2.5

	HOURS	RATE	AMOUNT
REGULAR	40.00	9.00	360.00
OVERTIME	5.5	13.50	74.25
TOTAL HOURS	45.5	TOTAL EARNINGS	434.25

Supervisor's OT Approval ___Joe Jensen___

Employee's Signature ___Sue Wetzel___

SECTION III

3.1
a. 0
b. 0
c. $1
d. $1
e. 0
f. 0
g. $17

h. $18
i. $55
j. $30
k. $29
l. $23
m. $42
n. $58

3.2

PAYROLL REGISTER for the Semimonthly Payroll Period Ended March 15, 20—

NO.	EMPLOYEE DATA			EARNINGS			DEDUCTIONS					NET PAY
	NAME	MARITAL STATUS	EXEMP.	REGULAR	OVERTIME	TOTAL	FEDERAL INCOME TAX	FICA	GROUP HEALTH INSURANCE	OTHER	TOTAL DEDUCTIONS	AMOUNT
1	Bentley, James	M	2	806 00		806 00	46 00	61 66			107 66	698 34
5	Clark, Chris	S	1	425 00		425 00	30 00	32 51			62 51	362 49
3	Day, Horace	M	3	751 00	60 00	811 00	29 00	62 04			91 04	719 96
6	Finch, Mike	M	1	570 00		570 00	28 00	43 61			71 61	498 39
2	Green, Jack	S	1	490 00	38 00	528 00	45 00	40 39			85 39	442 61
4	Howard, Mary	S	0	629 60	22 00	651 60	81 00	49 85			130 85	520 75
7	Lowe, Tom	M	1	859 60	22 75	882 35	76 00	67 50			143 50	738 85
12	Moore, Mary	M	3	815 00		815 00	29 00	62 35			91 35	723 65
11	North, Robert	S	1	687 00	32 00	719 00	72 00	55 00			127 00	592 00
10	Paul, Harry	M	3	768 00	11 00	779 00	23 00	59 59			82 59	696 41
8	Smith, Joe	S	0	592 00		592 00	72 00	45 29			117 29	474 71
9	Wilson, Joan	M	2	572 00	19 50	591 50	13 00	45 25			58 25	533 25
	Totals			7965 20	205 25	8170 45	544 00	625 04			1169 04	7001 41

SECTION IV

4.1

Employee Number	Regular Hours	Overtime Hours	Regular Rate	Regular Earnings	Overtime Earnings	Total Earnings
1	40	3	$7.50	*300.00*	*33.75*	*333.75*
2	40	8	8.25	*330.00*	*99.00*	*429.00*
3	40	0	6.00	*240.00*		*240.00*
4	35	0	5.75	*201.25*		*201.25*
5	40	6	6.75	*270.00*	*60.75*	*330.75*
6	29	0	8.50	*246.50*		*246.50*
7	40	2.5	9.25	*370.00*	*34.69*	*404.69*
8	32	0	7.00	*224.00*		*224.00*
9	40	1.75	7.25	*290.00*	*19.03*	*309.03*
10	39	0	9.45	*368.55*		*368.55*
11	40	3.75	8.35	*334.00*	*46.97*	*380.97*
12	40	1	5.50	*220.00*	*8.25*	*228.25*
13	40	8.5	5.15	*206.00*	*65.66*	*271.66*
14	40	10	6.80	*272.00*	*102.00*	*374.00*
15	40	1.5	6.30	*252.00*	*14.18*	*266.18*

4.2 Adult Check

4.3

<table>
<tr><td colspan="16" align="center">EMPLOYEE EARNINGS RECORD
for the Quarter Ended *March 31, 20—*</td></tr>
</table>

Howard Wilcox
910 Holly Drive
Binghamton, NY 13905

EMPLOYEE NO.: **45** MARITAL STATUS: **M**
POSITION: *Manager* ALLOWANCES: **3**
RATE OF PAY: **15.00** SSN: **123-45-6790**

PAY PERIOD		EARNINGS			DEDUCTIONS					ACCUMULATED EARNINGS	
PAY NO.	ENDED	REGULAR	OVERTIME	TOTAL	FEDERAL INCOME TAX	FICA	HEALTH INSURANCE	OTHER	TOTAL DEDUCTIONS	NET PAY	YEAR TO DATE
1	1-15	1200 00		1200 00	89 00	91 80	50 00	15 00	245 80	954 20	1200 00
2	1-31	1200 00	70 00	1270 00	98 00	97 16	50 00	15 00	260 16	1009 84	2470 00
3	2-15	1200 00		1200 00	89 00	91 80	50 00	15 00	245 80	954 20	3670 00
4	2-28	1200 00		1200 00	89 00	91 80	50 00	15 00	245 80	954 20	4870 00
5	3-15	1200 00	70 00	1270 00	98 00	97 16	50 00	15 00	260 16	1009 84	6140 00
6	3-31	1200 00		1200 00	89 00	91 80	50 00	15 00	245 80	954 20	7340 00
	Totals	7200 00	140 00	7340 00	552 00	561 52	300 00	90 00	1503 52	5836 48	

VOCABULARY

Employee Earnings Record – a form used to summarize payroll deductions and payments made to each individual employee.

Federal Unemployment Tax Act (FUTA) – a federal tax used for administration of state and federal unemployment programs.

Federal Insurance Contribution Act (FICA) – a law requiring employers and employees to pay taxes to the federal government to support the Social Security programs; the term "FICA" is also used to refer to the taxes themselves.

Merit Rating – a rating used to adjust an employer's state unemployment tax liability based upon a record of steady employment.

Pay Period – a period covered by a salary payment.

Payroll – all salaries and wages paid to employees.

Payroll Deductions – required and voluntary deductions from gross earnings to determine net pay.

Payroll Register – an accounting form that summarizes payroll information for all employees during a specific pay period.

Salary – a specified amount paid to an employee per month or per year.

State Unemployment Tax – a tax imposed by a state to pay benefits to the unemployed.

Wages – payment based on an hourly rate or a piecework basis.

SECTION I

1.1

JOURNAL							Page 5	
Date 20—	Account Title and Explanation	Doc No.	Post. Ref.	General Debit		General Credit		
Jan. 15	Salary Expense		570	4902	50			
	Employee Income Tax Payable		210				326	00
	FICA Tax Payable		220				303	96
	Medicare Tax Payable		230				71	10
	Cash	Ck132	110				4201	44

Account Title: Cash							Account No. 110		
Date 20—	Explanation	Post. Ref.	Debit		Credit		Balance		
							Debit		Credit
Jan. 1		✔	7871	00			7871	00	
15		J3			4201	44	3669	56	

Account Title: Employee Income Tax Payable							Account No. 210		
Date 20—	Explanation	Post. Ref.	Debit		Credit		Balance		
							Debit		Credit
Jan. 15		J3			326	00			326	00

Account Title: FICA Tax Payable							Account No. 220		
Date 20—	Explanation	Post. Ref.	Debit		Credit		Balance		
							Debit		Credit
Jan. 15		J3			303	96			303	96

Account Title: Medicare Tax Payable   **Account No.** 230

Date 20—		Explanation	Post. Ref.	Debit		Credit		Balance Debit		Balance Credit	
Jan.	15		J3			71	10			71	10

Account Title: Salary Expense   **Account No.** 570

Date 20—		Explanation	Post. Ref.	Debit		Credit		Balance Debit		Balance Credit	
Jan.	15		J3	4902	50			4902	50		

SECTION II

2.1 **Teacher's Note:** Until the student clearly grasps the concept of matching employer payroll taxes (FICA and Medicare) there may be some initial confusion when apparently duplicate ledger entries appear in these two accounts. You may wish to have the student label each entry as "Employee" and "Employer" the first few times he or she posts these entries. The examples shown below are in parentheses to indicate that this is an **optional** designation.

JOURNAL							Page 2	
Date 20—		Account Title and Explanation	Doc No.	Post. Ref.	General Debit		General Credit	
Dec.	31	Payroll Taxes Expense		550	285	42		
		FICA Tax Payable		220			169	26
		Medicare Tax Payable		230			39	59
		Unempl. Tax Pay.-Federal		240			9	88
		Unempl. Tax Pay.-State	M4	250			66	69

Account Title: FICA Tax Payable   **Account No. 220**

Date 20—		Explanation	Post. Ref.	Debit		Credit		Balance Debit		Balance Credit	
Dec.	15		✔							338	52
	31	(Employee)	J2			169	26			507	78
	31	(Employer)	J2			169	26			677	04

Account Title: Medicare Tax Payable   **Account No. 230**

Date 20—		Explanation	Post. Ref.	Debit		Credit		Balance Debit		Balance Credit	
Dec.	15		✔							79	18
	31	(Employee)	J2			39	59			118	77
	31	(Employer)	J2			39	59			158	36

Account Title: Unempl. Tax Payable – Federal   **Account No. 240**

Date 20—		Explanation	Post. Ref.	Debit		Credit		Balance Debit		Balance Credit	
Dec.	1		✔							39	52
	15		J2			9	88			49	40
	31		J2			9	88			59	28

SECTION II (CONT)

Account Title: *Unempl. Tax Payable – State*							Account No. *250*	
Date 20–		Explanation	Post. Ref.	Debit		Credit		Balance
							Debit	Credit
Dec.	1		✔					266 76
	15		J2			66 69		333 45
	31		J2			66 69		400 14

Account Title: *Payroll Taxes Expense*							Account No. *550*	
Date 20–		Explanation	Post. Ref.	Debit		Credit		Balance
							Debit	Credit
Dec.	15		J2	285 42				285 42
	31		J2	285 42				570 84

SECTION III

3.1

Payroll Tax	Employee	Employer
Federal Income Taxes	✔	
State Unemployment Taxes		✔
FICA (Social Security) Taxes	✔	✔
Federal Unemployment Taxes		✔
State Income Taxes	✔	
Medicare Taxes	✔	✔

3.2

Employee	Accumulated Earnings 10/31/20–	Total Earnings on 11/15/20–	Unemployment Taxable Earnings
Abelman, Adam	$10,200.00	$800.00	a. $ 0
Cain, Evelyn	6,400.00	800.00	b. 600.00
Isaacs, Jacob	2,890.00	350.00	c. 350.00
Jericho, Joshua	6,690.00	695.00	d. 310.00
Solomon, David	6,840.00	185.00	e. 160.00
TOTALS:	f. $33,020.00	g. $2,830.00	h. $1,420.00

3.3 a. $175.46   c. $ 11.36
     b. $ 41.04   d. $ 76.68

SECTION IV

4.1 *Teacher's Notes:*

1. No employee total earnings have exceeded the maximum tax base limit.

2. The Cash account is not complete. It reflects only the current payroll transactions. It is provided for posting practice only.

3. Make sure students *do not* skip lines between journal entries.

Date 20—		Account Title and Explanation	Doc No.	Post. Ref.	General Debit		General Credit	
Jan.	15	Salary Expense		570	5827	00		
		Employee Income Tax Pay.		210			684	00
		FICA Tax Payable		220			361	27
		Medicare Tax Payable		230			84	49
		United Way Payable		270			150	00
		Cash	Ck286	110			4547	24
	15	Payroll Taxes Expense		550	807	04		
		FICA Tax Payable		220			361	27
		Medicare Tax Payable		230			84	49
		Unempl. Tax Pay. – Federal		240			46	62
		Unempl. Tax Pay. – State	M3	250			314	66
	31	Salary Expense		570	4982	00		
		Employee Income Tax Pay.		210			597	00
		FICA Tax Payable		220			308	88
		Medicare Tax Payable		230			72	24
		United Way Payable		270			95	00
		Cash	Ck359	110			3908	88
	31	Payroll Taxes Expense		550	690	01		
		FICA Tax Payable		220			308	88
		Medicare Tax Payable		230			72	24
		Unempl. Tax Pay. – Federal		240			39	86
		Unempl. Tax Pay. – State	M6	250			269	03

JOURNAL   Page 1

Payroll Tax Summary Sheet January 15, 20–   *Memo #3*

	Debit	Credit
Payroll Taxes Expense	$807.04	
FICA Tax Payable		361.27
Medicare Tax Payable		84.49
Unemployment Tax Payable – Federal		46.62
Unemployment Tax Payable – State		314.66

Payroll Tax Summary Sheet January 31, 20–   *Memo #6*

	Debit	Credit
Payroll Taxes Expense	$690.01	
FICA Tax Payable		308.88
Medicare Tax Payable		72.24
Unemployment Tax Payable – Federal		39.86
Unemployment Tax Payable – State		269.03

Account Title: *Cash*   Account No. *110*

Date 20–		Explanation	Post. Ref.	Debit	Credit	Balance Debit	Balance Credit
Jan.	1		✔			10980 00	
	15		J1		4527 24	6432 76	
	31		J1		3908 88	2523 88	

Account Title: *Employee Income Tax Payable*   **Account No.** *210*

Date 20—		Explanation	Post. Ref.	Debit		Credit		Balance			
								Debit		Credit	
Jan.	15		J1			684	00			684	00
	31		J1			597	00			1281	00

Account Title: *FICA Tax Payable*   **Account No.** *220*

Date 20—		Explanation	Post. Ref.	Debit		Credit		Balance			
								Debit		Credit	
Jan.	15		J1			361	27			361	27
	15		J1			361	27			722	54
	31		J1			308	88			1031	42
	31		J1			308	88			1340	30

Account Title: *Medicare Tax Payable*   **Account No.** *230*

Date 20—		Explanation	Post. Ref.	Debit		Credit		Balance			
								Debit		Credit	
Jan.	15		J1			84	49			84	49
	15		J1			84	49			168	98
	31		J1			72	24			241	22
	31		J1			72	24			313	46

Account Title: *Unempl. Tax Payable – Federal*   **Account No.** *240*

Date 20—		Explanation	Post. Ref.	Debit		Credit		Balance			
								Debit		Credit	
Jan.	15		J1			46	62			46	62
	31		J1			39	86			86	48

Account Title: *Unempl. Tax Payable – State*   **Account No.** *250*

Date 20—		Explanation	Post. Ref.	Debit		Credit		Balance			
								Debit		Credit	
Jan.	15		J1			314	66			314	66
	31		J1			269	03			583	69

Account Title: *United Way Payable*   **Account No.** *270*

Date 20—		Explanation	Post. Ref.	Debit		Credit		Balance			
								Debit		Credit	
Jan.	15		J1			150	00			150	00
	31		J1			95	00			245	00

Account Title: *Payroll Taxes Expense*   **Account No.** *550*

Date 20—		Explanation	Post. Ref.	Debit		Credit		Balance			
								Debit		Credit	
Jan.	15		J1	807	04			807	04		
	31		J1	690	01			1497	05		

Account Title: *Salary Expense*   **Account No.** *570*

Date 20—		Explanation	Post. Ref.	Debit		Credit		Balance			
								Debit		Credit	
Jan.	15		J1	5827	00			5827	00		
	31		J1	4982	00			10809	00		

4.2 ***Teacher's Notes:***

1. No employee total earnings have exceeded the maximum tax base limit.

2. The July 1 balances that appear in the general ledger are carried over from the previous month.

3. The Cash account is not complete. It reflects only the current payroll transactions. It is provided for posting practice only.

Payroll Tax Summary Sheet July 15, 20–		*Memo #4*
	Debit	*Credit*
Payroll Taxes Expense	*$444.86*	
FICA Tax Payable		*199.14*
Medicare Tax Payable		*46.57*
Unemployment Tax Payable – Federal		*25.70*
Unemployment Tax Payable – State		*173.45*

Payroll Tax Summary Sheet July 31, 20–		*Memo #8*
	Debit	*Credit*
Payroll Taxes Expense	*$440.43*	
FICA Tax Payable		*197.16*
Medicare Tax Payable		*46.11*
Unemployment Tax Payable – Federal		*25.44*
Unemployment Tax Payable – State		*171.72*

4.2   **Teacher's Note:** Make sure students *do not* skip lines between journal entries.

Date 20—		Account Title and Explanation	Doc No.	Post. Ref.	General Debit		General Credit	
July	15	*Employee Income Tax Payable*		210	896	00		
		FICA Tax Payable		220	376	84		
		Medicare Tax Payable		230	88	13		
		Cash	Ck148	110			1360	97
	15	*Salary Expense*		570	3212	00		
		Employee Income Tax Pay.		210			489	00
		FICA Tax Payable		220			199	14
		Medicare Tax Payable		230			46	57
		United Way Payable		260			128	48
		Cash	Ck149	110			2348	81
	15	*Payroll Taxes Expense*		550	444	86		
		FICA Tax Payable		220			199	14
		Medicare Tax Payable		230			46	57
		Unempl. Tax Pay. – Federal		240			25	70
		Unempl. Tax Pay. – State	M4	250			173	45
	31	*Unempl. Tax Pay. – Federal*		240	159	84		
		Cash	Ck150	110			159	84
	31	*Unempl. Tax Pay. – State*		250	887	92		
		Cash	Ck151	110			887	92
	31	*United Way Payable*		260	299	20		
		Cash	Ck152	110			299	20
	31	*Salary Expense*		570	3180	00		
		Employee Income Tax Pay.		210			439	00
		FICA Tax Payable		220			197	16
		Medicare Tax Payable		230			46	11
		United Way Payable		260			100	00
		Cash	Ck153	110			2397	73
	31	*Payroll Taxes Expense*		550	440	43		
		FICA Tax Payable		220			197	16
		Medicare Tax Payable		230			46	11
		Unempl. Tax Pay. – Federal		240			25	44
		Unempl. Tax Pay. – State	M8	250			171	72

JOURNAL — Page 4

Account Title: *Cash*   **Account No.** *110*

Date 20—		Explanation	Post. Ref.	Debit		Credit		Balance Debit		Balance Credit	
July	1		✔					15980	00		
	15		J4			1360	97	14529	28		
	15		J4			2348	81	12180	47		
	31		J4			159	84	12020	63		
	31		J4			887	92	11132	71		
	31		J4			299	20	10833	51		
	31		J4			2397	73	8435	78		

Account Title: *Employee Income Tax Payable*   **Account No.** *210*

Date 20—		Explanation	Post. Ref.	Debit		Credit		Balance Debit		Balance Credit	
July	1		✔							896	00
	15		J4	896	00					—	
	15		J4			489	00			489	00
	31		J4			439	00			928	00

Account Title: *FICA Tax Payable*   **Account No.** *220*

Date 20—		Explanation	Post. Ref.	Debit		Credit		Balance Debit		Balance Credit	
July	1		✔							376	84
	15		J4	376	84					—	
	15		J4			199	14			199	14
	31		J4			199	14			398	28
	31		J4			197	16			595	44
	31		J4			197	16			792	60

Account Title: *Medicare Tax Payable*								Account No. *230*	
Date 20—		Explanation	Post. Ref.	Debit		Credit		Balance	
								Debit	Credit
July	1		✔						88 13
	15		J4	88 13					—
	15		J4			46 57			46 57
	31		J4			46 57			93 14
	31		J4			46 11			139 25
	31		J4			46 11			185 36

Account Title: *Unempl. Tax Payable – Federal*								Account No. *240*	
Date 20—		Explanation	Post. Ref.	Debit		Credit		Balance	
								Debit	Credit
July	1		✔						159 84
	15		J4			25 70			185 54
	15		J4	159 84					25 70
	31		J4			25 44			51 14

Account Title: *Unempl. Tax Payable – State*								Account No. *250*	
Date 20—		Explanation	Post. Ref.	Debit		Credit		Balance	
								Debit	Credit
July	1		✔						887 92
	15		J4			173 45			1061 37
	31		J4	887 92					173 45
	31		J4			171 72			345 17

Account Title: *Payroll Taxes Expense* **Account No.** *550*

Date 20—		Explanation	Post. Ref.	Debit		Credit		Balance			
								Debit		Credit	
July	15		J4	444	86			444	86		
	31		J4	440	43			885	29		

Account Title: *Salary Expense* **Account No.** *570*

Date 20—		Explanation	Post. Ref.	Debit		Credit		Balance			
								Debit		Credit	
July.	15		J4	3212	00			3212	00		
	31		J4	3180	00			6392	00		

Account Title: *United Way Payable* **Account No.** *260*

Date 20—		Explanation	Post. Ref.	Debit		Credit		Balance			
								Debit		Credit	
July	1		✔							299	20
	15		J4			128	48			427	68
	31		J4	299	20					128	48
	31		J4			100	00			228	48

OPTIONAL EXERCISES FOR EXTRA CREDIT

Teacher's Notes:

1. No employee total earnings have exceeded the maximum tax base limit.

2. The September 1 balances that appear in the general ledger are carried over from the previous month.

3. The Cash account is not complete. It reflects only the current payroll transactions. It is provided for posting practice only.

4. The temporary accounts that are normally closed at the end of the month are not closed for this exercise. They are provided for posting practice only.

5. Make sure the students do not skip lines between the journal entries.

6. Remember to keep journal entries together on a journal page. Do not divide an entry between journal pages.

Student Instructions:

Have the student(s) complete this activity in the following order:

1. Journalize and post the transactions for September 15th. Begin with page 8 of the journal.

2. Journalize and post the transactions for September 30th.

3. Journalize and post the transactions for October 15th.

4. Journalize and post the transactions for October 31st.

Grading instructions:

Each item in this activity counts as ***one-half*** point. All journal page numbers, dates (year, month and day), account titles, document numbers, posting reference account numbers, amounts, rulings, etc. each count as single a item. This exercise has 546 individual items. ***Total Points – 273***

Payroll Tax Expense Summaries	20 points
Journal Entries	242 points
Ledger Accounts	<u>284 points</u>
Total Points	546 points

546 ÷ 2 = 273 points

Payroll Tax Summary Sheet September 15, 20–   *Memo #8*

	Debit	Credit
Payroll Taxes Expense	$906.95	
FICA Tax Payable		406.00
Medicare Tax Payable		94.95
Unemployment Tax Payable – Federal		52.39
Unemployment Tax Payable – State		353.61

Payroll Tax Summary Sheet September 30, 20–   *Memo #9*

	Debit	Credit
Payroll Taxes Expense	$915.13	
FICA Tax Payable		409.66
Medicare Tax Payable		95.81
Unemployment Tax Payable – Federal		52.86
Unemployment Tax Payable – State		356.80

Payroll Tax Summary Sheet October 15, 20–   *Memo #10*

	Debit	Credit
Payroll Taxes Expense	$929.34	
FICA Tax Payable		416.02
Medicare Tax Payable		97.30
Unemployment Tax Payable – Federal		53.68
Unemployment Tax Payable – State		362.34

Payroll Tax Summary Sheet October 31, 20–   *Memo #11*

	Debit	Credit
Payroll Taxes Expense	$891.94	
FICA Tax Payable		399.28
Medicare Tax Payable		93.38
Unemployment Tax Payable – Federal		51.52
Unemployment Tax Payable – State		347.76

Date 20—		Account Title and Explanation	Doc No.	Post. Ref.	General Debit		General Credit	
Sept.	15	*Employee Income Tax Payable*		210	1959	00		
		FICA Tax Payable		220	1599	60		
		Medicare Tax Payable		230	347	55		
		Cash	Ck678	110			3906	15
	15	*Salary Expense*		570	6548	39		
		Employee Income Tax Pay.		210			982	00
		FICA Tax Payable		220			406	00
		Medicare Tax Payable		230			94	95
		U.S. Savings Bonds Payable		260			126	00
		United Way Payable		270			88	50
		Cash	Ck679	110			4850	94
	15	*Payroll Taxes Expense*		550	906	95		
		FICA Tax Payable		220			406	00
		Medicare Tax Payable		230			94	95
		Unempl. Tax Pay. – Federal		240			52	39
		Unempl. Tax Pay. – State	M8	250			353	61
	15	*U.S. Savings Bonds Payable*		260	350	00		
		Cash	Ck680	110			350	00
	15	*United Way Payable*		270	114	00		
		Cash	Ck681	110			114	00
	30	*Salary Expense*		570	6607	41		
		Employee Income Tax Pay.		210			997	00
		FICA Tax Payable		220			409	66
		Medicare Tax Payable		230			95	81
		U.S. Savings Bonds Payable		260			100	00
		United Way Payable		270			81	00
		Cash	Ck682	110			4923	24
	30	*Payroll Taxes Expense*		550	915	13		
		FICA Tax Payable		220			409	66
		Medicare Tax Payable		230			95	81
		Unempl. Tax Pay. – Federal		240			52	86
		Unempl. Tax Pay. – State	M9	250			356	80

JOURNAL — Page 8

		JOURNAL					Page 9	
Date		Account Title and Explanation	Doc No.	Post. Ref.	General Debit		General Credit	
Oct.	15	Employee Income Tax Payable		210	1979	00		
		FICA Tax Payable		220	1631	32		
		Medicare Tax Payable		230	381	52		
		Cash	Ck683	110			3991	84
	15	Salary Expense		570	6710	00		
		Employee Income Tax Pay.		210			1082	00
		FICA Tax Payable		220			416	02
		Medicare Tax Payable		230			97	30
		U.S. Savings Bonds Payable		260			75	00
		United Way Payable		270			85	00
		Cash	Ck684	110			4954	68
	15	Payroll Taxes Expense		550	929	34		
		FICA Tax Payable		220			416	02
		Medicare Tax Payable		230			97	30
		Unempl. Tax Pay. – Federal		240			53	68
		Unempl. Tax Pay. – State	M10	250			362	34
	15	U.S. Savings Bonds Payable		260	226	00		
		Cash	Ck685	110			226	00
	15	United Way Payable		270	169	50		
		Cash	Ck686	110			169	50
	31	Salary Expense		570	6440	00		
		Employee Income Tax Pay.		210			897	00
		FICA Tax Payable		220			399	28
		Medicare Tax Payable		230			93	38
		U.S. Savings Bonds Payable		260			150	00
		United Way Payable		270			65	00
		Cash	Ck687	110			4835	34
	31	Payroll Taxes Expense		550	891	94		
		FICA Tax Payable		220			399	28
		Medicare Tax Payable		230			93	38
		Unempl. Tax Pay. – Federal		240			51	52
		Unempl. Tax Pay. – State	M11	250			347	76
	31	Unempl. Tax Pay. – Federal		240	262	55		
		Cash	Ck688	110			262	55
	31	Unempl. Tax Pay. – State		250	1707	01		
		Cash	Ck689	110			1707	01

Account Title: *Cash*   **Account No.** *110*

Date		Explanation	Post. Ref.	Debit		Credit		Balance			
								Debit		Credit	
Sept.	1		✔					41044	95		
	15		J8			3906	15	37138	80		
	15		J8			4850	94	32287	46		
	15		J8			350	00	31937	86		
	15		J8			114	00	31823	86		
	30		J8			4923	94	26899	92		
Oct.	15		J9			3991	84	22908	08		
	15		J9			4954	68	17953	40		
	15		J9			226	00	17727	40		
	15		J9			169	50	17557	90		
	31		J9			4835	34	12722	56		
	31		J9			262	55	12460	01		
	31		J9			1707	01	10753	00		

Account Title: *Employee Income Tax Payable*   **Account No.** *210*

Date		Explanation	Post. Ref.	Debit		Credit		Balance			
								Debit		Credit	
Sept.	1		✔							1959	00
	15		J8	1959	00					—	
	15		J8			982	00			982	00
	30		J8			997	00			1979	00
Oct.	15		J9	1979	00					—	
	15		J9			1082	00			1082	00
	31		J9			897	00			1979	00

Account Title: FICA Tax Payable   **Account No.** 220

Date		Explanation	Post. Ref.	Debit		Credit		Balance			
								Debit		Credit	
Sept.	1		✔							1599	60
	15		J8	1599	60					———	
	15		J8			406	00			406	00
	15		J8			406	00			812	00
	30		J8			409	66			1221	66
	30		J8			409	66			1631	32
Oct.	15		J9	1631	32					———	
	15		J9			416	02			416	02
	15		J9			416	02			832	04
	31		J9			399	28			1231	32
	31		J9			399	28			1630	60

Account Title: Medicare Tax Payable   **Account No.** 230

Date		Explanation	Post. Ref.	Debit		Credit		Balance			
								Debit		Credit	
Sept.	1		✔							347	55
	15		J8	347	55						
	15		J8			94	95			94	95
	15		J8			94	95			189	90
	30		J8			95	81			285	71
	30		J8			95	81			381	52
Oct.	15		J9	381	52						
	15		J9			97	30			97	30
	15		J9			97	30			194	60
	31		J9			93	38			287	98
	31		J9			93	38			381	36

Account Title: *Unempl. Tax Payable – Federal*							Account No. *240*	
Date 20—		Explanation	Post. Ref.	Debit		Credit		Balance
							Debit	Credit
Sept.	1		✔					157	30
	15		J8			52	39		209	69
	30		J8			52	86		262	55
Oct.	15		J9			53	68		316	23
	31		J9			51	52		367	75
	31		J9	262	55				105	20

Account Title: *Unempl. Tax Payable – State*							Account No. *250*	
Date 20—		Explanation	Post. Ref.	Debit		Credit		Balance
							Debit	Credit
Sept.	1		✔					996	60
	15		J8			353	61		1350	21
	30		J8			356	80		1707	01
Oct.	15		J9			362	34		2069	35
	31		J9			347	76		2417	11
	31		J9	1707	01				710	10

Account Title: *U. S. Savings Bonds Payable*							Account No. *260*	
Date 20—		Explanation	Post. Ref.	Debit		Credit		Balance
							Debit	Credit
Sept.	1		✔					350	00
	15		J8			126	00		476	00
	15		J8	350	00				126	00
	30		J8			100	00		226	00
Oct.	15		J9			75	00		301	00
	15		J9	226	00				75	00
	31		J9			150	00		225	00

Account Title: *United Way Payable*   **Account No.** *270*

Date 20—		Explanation	Post. Ref.	Debit		Credit		Balance Debit		Balance Credit	
Sept.	1		✔							114	00
	15		J8			88	50			202	50
	15		J8	114	00					88	50
	30		J8			81	00			169	50
Oct.	15		J9			85	00			254	50
	15		J9	169	50					85	00
	31		J9			65	00			150	00

Account Title: *Payroll Taxes Expense*   **Account No.** *550*

Date 20—		Explanation	Post. Ref.	Debit		Credit		Balance Debit		Balance Credit	
Sept.	15		J8	906	95			906	95		
	30		J8	915	13			1822	08		
Oct.	15		J9	929	34			2751	42		
	31		J9	891	94			3643	36		

Account Title: *Salary Expense*   **Account No.** *570*

Date 20—		Explanation	Post. Ref.	Debit		Credit		Balance Debit		Balance Credit	
Sept.	15		J8	6548	39			6548	39		
	30		J8	6607	41			13155	80		
Oct.	15		J9	6710	00			19865	80		
	31		J9	6440	00			26305	80		

126 Individual Items: Total Points – 63

Teacher's Note: *Individual items in each activity of this LIFEPAC count as* **one-half** *point, including document numbers, account numbers, titles, amounts, dates, page numbers, headings, rulings, etc.*

JOURNAL								**Page 1**
Date 20—		Account Title and Explanation	Doc No.	Post. Ref.	General Debit		General Credit	
Mar.	1	Cash		110	22000	00		
		Olive Larson, Capital	R1	310			22000	00
	2	Office Equipment		160	1500	00		
		Olive Larson, Capital	M1	310			1500	00
	3	Automobile		150	17950	00		
		First City Bank		240			10150	00
		Cash	Ck101	110			7800	00
	4	Supplies		130	1800	00		
		Cash	Ck102	110			1800	00
	4	Rent Expense		560	1250	00		
		Cash	Ck103	110			1250	00
	4	Miscellaneous Expense		540	6	80		
		Cash	Ck104	110			6	80
	4	Cash		110	2675	00		
		Tour Fees	T4	410			2675	00
	6	Prepaid Insurance		140	3280	00		
		Cash	Ck105	110			3280	00
	6	Supplies		130	895	00		
		A to Z Office Supply	M2	210			895	00
	7	Utilities Expense		590	235	00		
		Cash	Ck106	110			235	00
	7	Automobile Expense		520	17	90		
		Cash	Ck107	110			17	90
	8	Miscellaneous Expense		540	98	00		
		Cash	Ck108	110			98	00
	9	Automobile Expense		520	495	00		
		Cash	Ck109	110			495	00
	9	Olive Larson, Drawing		320	850	00		
		Cash	Ck110	110			850	00
	10	A to Z Office Supply		210	450	00		
		Cash	Ck111	110			450	00

125 Individual Items: Total Points – 62.5

		Account Title and Explanation	Doc No.	Post. Ref.	General Debit		General Credit	
JOURNAL							**Page 2**	
Date 20—		Account Title and Explanation	Doc No.	Post. Ref.	General Debit		General Credit	
Mar.	10	Utilities Expense		590	790	00		
		Cash	Ck112	110			790	00
	11	Cash		110	7690	00		
		Tour Fees	T11	410			7690	00
	13	Miscellaneous Expense		540	108	00		
		Cash	Ck113	110			108	00
	13	Advertising Expense		510	975	00		
		Cash	Ck114	110			975	00
	13	Miscellaneous Expense		540	110	00		
		Cash	Ck115	110			110	00
	13	Automobile Expense		520	23	00		
		Cash	Ck116	110			23	00
	14	Advertising Expense		510	83	50		
		Cash	Ck117	110			83	50
	14	A to Z Office Supply		210	445	00		
		Cash	Ck118	110			445	00
	15	Supplies		130	695	00		
		A to Z Office Supply	M3	210			695	00
	15	Salary Expense		570	1600	00		
		Employee Income Tax Pay.		220			174	00
		FICA Tax Payable		230			99	20
		Medicare Tax Payable		250			23	20
		Cash	Ck119	110			1303	60
	15	Payroll Taxes Expense		550	204	00		
		FICA Tax Payable		230			99	20
		Medicare Tax Payable		250			23	20
		Unempl. Tax Payable – Fed.		260			12	80
		Unempl. Tax Payable – State	M5	270			68	80
	16	Miscellaneous Expense		540	19	80		
		Cash	Ck120	110			19	80
	16	First City Bank		240	350	00		
		Cash	Ck121	110			350	00

131 Individual Items: Total Points – 65.5

Date 20—		Account Title and Explanation	Doc No.	Post. Ref.	General Debit		General Credit	
Mar.	17	Miscellaneous Expense		540	87	90		
		Cash	Ck122	110			87	90
	17	Prepaid Insurance		140	1860	00		
		Cash	Ck123	110			1860	00
	18	Olive Larson, Drawing		320	850	00		
		Cash	Ck124	110			850	00
	18	Automobile Expense		520	79	95		
		Cash	Ck125	110			79	95
	18	Cash		110	5670	00		
		Tour Fees	T18	410			5670	00
	18	Miscellaneous Expense		540	158	00		
		Cash	Ck126	110			158	00
	20	Utilities Expense		590	367	00		
		Cash	Ck127	110			367	00
	20	Miscellaneous Expense		540	110	00		
		Cash	Ck128	110			110	00
	21	Automobile Expense		520	82	50		
		Cash	Ck129	110			82	50
	21	A to Z Office Supply		210	250	00		
		Cash	Ck130	110			250	00
	22	Office Equipment		160	1195	00		
		Cash	Ck131	110			1195	00
	23	Advertising Expense		510	60	00		
		Cash	Ck132	110			60	00
	23	Miscellaneous Expense		540	7	50		
		Cash	Ck133	110			7	50
	24	Supplies		130	295	00		
		Cash	Ck134	110			295	00
	25	Cash		110	3895	00		
		Tour Fees	T25	410			3895	00
	27	Miscellaneous Expense		540	318	00		
		Cash	Ck135	110			318	00

JOURNAL — Page 3

85 Individual Items: Total Points – 42.5

JOURNAL								Page *4*
Date 20—	Account Title and Explanation	Doc No.	Post. Ref.	General Debit		General Credit		
Mar. 28	*Automobile Expense*		520	27	00			
	Cash	*Ck136*	110			27	00	
30	*Olive Larson, Drawing*		320	850	00			
	Cash	*Ck137*	110			850	00	
30	*Miscellaneous Expense*		540	9	75			
	Cash	*M9*	110			9	75	
30	*Cash*		110	1975	00			
	Tour Fees	*T31*	410			1975	00	
30	*Petty Cash*		120	300	00			
	Cash	*Ck138*	110			300	00	
30	*Miscellaneous Expense*		540	682	00			
	Cash	*M10*	110			682	00	
31	*Salary Expense*		570	1800	00			
	Employee Income Tax Pay.		220			188	00	
	FICA Tax Payable		230			111	60	
	Medicare Tax Payable		250			26	10	
	Cash	*Ck139*	110			1474	30	
31	*Payroll Taxes Expense*		550	229	50			
	FICA Tax Payable		230			111	60	
	Medicare Tax Payable		250			26	10	
	Unempl. Tax Payable – Fed.		260			14	40	
	Unempl. Tax Payable – State	*M12*	270			77	40	

71 Individual Items: Total Points – 35.5

				JOURNAL			Page 5	
Date 20—		Account Title and Explanation	Doc No.	Post. Ref.	General Debit		General Credit	
		Adjusting Entries						
Mar.	31	Supplies Expense		580	2505	00		
		Supplies		130			2505	00
	31	Insurance Expense		530	3110	00		
		Prepaid Insurance		140			3110	00
		Closing Entries						
	31	Tour Fees		410	21905	00		
		Income Summary		330			21905	00
	31	Income Summary		330	15650	10		
		Advertising Expense		510			1118	50
		Automobile Expense		520			725	35
		Insurance Expense		530			3110	00
		Miscellaneous Expense		540			1715	75
		Payroll Taxes Expense		550			433	50
		Rent Expense		560			1250	00
		Salary Expense		570			3400	00
		Supplies Expense		580			2505	00
		Utilities Expense		590			1392	00
	31	Income Summary		330	6254	90		
		Olive Larson, Capital		310			6254	90
	31	Olive Larson, Capital		310	2550	00		
		Olive Larson, Drawing		320			2550	00

132 Individual Items: Total Points – 66

Account Title: *Cash*									Account No. *110*	
Date 20—		Explanation	Post. Ref.	Debit		Credit		Balance		
								Debit		Credit
Mar.	1		J1	22000	00			22000	00	
	3		J1			7800	00	14200	00	
	4		J1			1800	00	12400	00	
	4		J1			1250	00	11150	00	
	4		J1			6	80	11143	20	
	4		J1	2675	00			13818	20	
	6		J1			3280	00	10538	20	
	7		J1			235	00	10303	20	
	7		J1			17	90	10285	30	
	8		J1			98	00	10187	30	
	9		J1			495	00	9692	30	
	9		J1			850	00	8842	30	
	10		J1			450	00	8392	30	
	10		J2			790	00	7602	30	
	11		J2	7690	00			15292	30	
	13		J2			108	00	15184	30	
	13		J2			975	00	14209	30	
	13		J2			110	00	14099	30	
	13		J2			23	00	14076	30	
	14		J2			83	50	13992	80	
	14		J2			445	00	13547	80	
	15		J2			1303	60	12244	20	
	16		J2			19	80	12224	40	
	16		J2			350	00	11874	40	
	17		J3			87	90	11786	50	
	17		J3			1860	00	9926	50	
	18		J3			850	00	9076	50	
	18		J3			79	95	8996	55	
	18		J3	5670	00			14666	55	
	18		J3			158	00	14508	55	
	20		J3			367	00	14141	55	
	20		J3			110	00	14031	55	

76 Individual Items: Total Points – 38

Account Title: *Cash*										Account No. *110*			
Date 20—		Explanation	Post. Ref.	Debit		Credit		Balance					
								Debit			Credit		
Mar.	20		✔					14031	55			
	21		J3			82	50	13949	05			
	21		J3			250	00	13699	05			
	22		J3			1195	00	12504	05			
	23		J3			60	00	12444	05			
	23		J3			7	50	12436	55			
	24		J3			295	00	12141	55			
	25		J3	3895	00			16036	55			
	27		J3			318	00	15718	55			
	28		J4			27	00	15691	55			
	30		J4			850	00	14841	55			
	30		J4			9	75	14831	80			
	30		J4	1975	00			16806	80			
	30		J4			300	00	16506	80			
	30		J4			682	00	15824	80			
	31		J4			1474	30	14350	50			

Account Title: *Petty Cash*										Account No. *120*			
Date 20—		Explanation	Post. Ref.	Debit		Credit		Balance					
								Debit			Credit		
Mar.	31		J4	300	00			300	00			

48 Individual Items: Total Points – 24

Account Title: *Supplies*							Account No. *130*	

Date 20—		Explanation	Post. Ref.	Debit		Credit		Balance			
								Debit		Credit	
Mar.	4		J1	1800	00			1800	00		
	6		J1	895	00			2695	00		
	15		J2	695	00			3390	00		
	24		J3	295	00			3685	00		
	31		J5			2505	00	1180	00		

Account Title: *Prepaid Insurance*							Account No. *140*	

Date 20—		Explanation	Post. Ref.	Debit		Credit		Balance			
								Debit		Credit	
Mar.	6		J1	3280	00			3280	00		
	17		J3	1860	00			5140	00		
	31		J5			3110	00	2030	00		

Account Title: *Automobile*							Account No. *150*	

Date 20—		Explanation	Post. Ref.	Debit		Credit		Balance			
								Debit		Credit	
Mar.	3		J1	17950	00			17950	00		

48 Individual Items: Total Points – 24

Account Title: *Office Equipment*   **Account No.** *160*

Date 20—		Explanation	Post. Ref.	Debit		Credit		Balance Debit		Balance Credit	
Mar.	2		J1	1500	00			1500	00		
	22		J3	1195	00			2695	00		

Account Title: *A to Z Office Supply*   **Account No.** *210*

Date 20—		Explanation	Post. Ref.	Debit		Credit		Balance Debit		Balance Credit	
Mar.	6		J1			895	00			895	00
	10		J1	450	00					445	00
	14		J2	445	00					—	
	15		J2			695	00			695	00
	21		J3	250	00					445	00

Account Title: *Employee Income Tax Payable*   **Account No.** *220*

Date 20—		Explanation	Post. Ref.	Debit		Credit		Balance Debit		Balance Credit	
Mar.	15		J2			174	00			174	00
	31		J4			188	00			362	00

52 Individual Items: Total Points – 26

Account Title: *FICA Tax Payable*								Account No. *230*	
Date 20—		Explanation	Post. Ref.	Debit		Credit		Balance	
								Debit	Credit
Mar.	15		J2			99	20		99	20
	15		J2			99	20		198	40
	31		J4			111	60		310	00
	31		J4			111	60		421	60

Account Title: *First City Bank*								Account No. *240*	
Date 20—		Explanation	Post. Ref.	Debit		Credit		Balance	
								Debit	Credit
Mar.	3		J1			10150	00		10150	00
	16		J2	350	00				9800	00

Account Title: *Medicare Tax Payable*								Account No. *250*	
Date 20—		Explanation	Post. Ref.	Debit		Credit		Balance	
								Debit	Credit
Mar.	15		J2			23	20		23	20
	15		J2			23	20		46	40
	31		J4			26	10		72	50
	31		J4			26	10		98	60

44 Individual Items: Total Points – 22

Account Title: *Unemployment Tax Payable – Federal*   **Account No. 260**

Date 20—		Explanation	Post. Ref.	Debit		Credit		Balance			
								Debit		Credit	
Mar.	15		J2			12	80			12	80
	31		J4			14	40			27	20

Account Title: *Unemployment Tax Payable – State*   **Account No. 270**

Date 20—		Explanation	Post. Ref.	Debit		Credit		Balance			
								Debit		Credit	
Mar.	15		J2			68	80			68	80
	31		J4			77	40			146	20

Account Title: *Olive Larson, Capital*   **Account No. 310**

Date 20—		Explanation	Post. Ref.	Debit		Credit		Balance			
								Debit		Credit	
Mar.	1		J1			22000	00			22000	00
	2		J1			1500	00			23500	00
	31		J5			6254	90			29754	90
	31		J5	2550	00					27204	90

64 Individual Items: Total Points – 32

| Account Title: *Olive Larson, Drawing* | | | | | | Account No. 320 | | | |

Date 20—		Explanation	Post. Ref.	Debit		Credit		Balance			
								Debit		Credit	
Mar.	9		J1	850	00			850	00		
	18		J3	850	00			1700	00		
	30		J4	850	00			2550	00		
	31		J5			2550	00	———			

| Account Title: *Income Summary* | | | | | | Account No. 330 | | | |

Date 20—		Explanation	Post. Ref.	Debit		Credit		Balance			
								Debit		Credit	
Mar.	31		J5			21905	00			21905	00
	31		J5	15650	10					6254	90
	31		J5	6254	90					———	

| Account Title: *Tour Fees* | | | | | | Account No. 410 | | | |

Date 20—		Explanation	Post. Ref.	Debit		Credit		Balance			
								Debit		Credit	
Mar.	4		J1			2675	00			2675	00
	11		J2			7690	00			10365	00
	18		J3			5670	00			16035	00
	25		J3			3895	00			19930	00
	30		J4			1975	00			21905	00
	31		J5	21905	00			———			

64 Individual Items: Total Points – 32

Account Title: *Advertising Expense*   **Account No. 510**

Date 20—		Explanation	Post. Ref.	Debit		Credit		Balance Debit		Credit	
Mar.	13		J2	975	00			975	00		
	14		J2	83	50			1058	50		
	23		J3	60	00			1118	50		
	31		J5			1118	50	———			

Account Title: *Automobile Expense*   **Account No. 520**

Date 20—		Explanation	Post. Ref.	Debit		Credit		Balance Debit		Credit	
Mar.	7		J1	17	90			17	90		
	9		J1	495	00			512	90		
	13		J2	23	00			535	90		
	18		J3	79	95			615	85		
	21		J3	82	50			698	35		
	28		J4	27	00			725	35		
	31		J5			725	35	———			

Account Title: *Insurance Expense*   **Account No. 530**

Date 20—		Explanation	Post. Ref.	Debit		Credit		Balance Debit		Credit	
Mar.	31		J5	3110	00			3110	00		
	31		J5			3110	00	———			

84 Individual Items: Total Points – 42

Account Title: *Miscellaneous Expense*   **Account No.** *540*

Date 20—		Explanation	Post. Ref.	Debit		Credit		Balance			
								Debit		Credit	
Mar.	*4*		*J1*	6	80			6	80		
	8		*J1*	98	00			104	80		
	13		*J2*	108	00			212	80		
	13		*J2*	110	00			322	80		
	16		*J2*	19	80			342	60		
	17		*J3*	87	90			430	50		
	18		*J3*	158	00			588	50		
	20		*J3*	110	00			698	50		
	23		*J3*	7	50			706	00		
	27		*J3*	318	00			1024	00		
	30		*J4*	9	75			1033	75		
	30		*J4*	682	00			1715	75		
	31		*J5*			1715	75	—	—		

Account Title: *Payroll Taxes Expense*   **Account No.** *550*

Date 20—		Explanation	Post. Ref.	Debit		Credit		Balance			
								Debit		Credit	
Mar.	*15*		*J2*	204	00			204	00		
	31		*J4*	229	50			433	50		
	31		*J5*			433	50	—	—		

Account Title: *Rent Expense*   **Account No.** *560*

Date 20—		Explanation	Post. Ref.	Debit		Credit		Balance			
								Debit		Credit	
Mar.	*4*		*J1*	1250	00			1250	00		
	31		*J5*			1250	00	—	—		

48 Individual Items: Total Points – 24

Account Title: *Salary Expense*								Account No. *570*	
Date 20—		Explanation	Post. Ref.	Debit		Credit		Balance	
								Debit	Credit
Mar.	15		J2	1600	00			1600	00	
	31		J4	1800	00			3400	00	
	31		J5			3400	00	———	

Account Title: *Supplies Expense*								Account No. *580*	
Date 20—		Explanation	Post. Ref.	Debit		Credit		Balance	
								Debit	Credit
Mar.	31		J5	2505	00			2505	00	
	31		J5			2505	00	———	

Account Title: *Utilities Expense*								Account No. *590*	
Date 20—		Explanation	Post. Ref.	Debit		Credit		Balance	
								Debit	Credit
Mar.	7		J1	235	00			235	00	
	10		J2	790	00			1025	00	
	20		J3	367	00			1392	00	
	31		J5			1392	00	———	

Accounting LIFEPAC 10

77 Individual Items: Total Points – 38.5

PAYROLL REGISTER for the Weekly Payroll Period Ended March 15, 20—

EMPLOYEE DATA				EARNINGS			DEDUCTIONS					NET PAY
NO.	NAME	MARITAL STATUS	EXEMP.	REGULAR	OVERTIME	TOTAL	FEDERAL INCOME TAX	FICA	MEDICARE	OTHER	TOTAL DEDUCTIONS	AMOUNT
1	Baker, Andrea	S	1	800 00		800 00	87 00	49 60	11 60		148 20	651 80
2	Craig, Sommer	S	1	800 00		800 00	87 00	49 60	11 60		148 20	651 80
	Totals			1600 00		1600 00	174 00	99 20	23 20		296 40	1303 60

PAYROLL REGISTER for the Weekly Payroll Period Ended March 31, 20—

EMPLOYEE DATA				EARNINGS			DEDUCTIONS					NET PAY
NO.	NAME	MARITAL STATUS	EXEMP.	REGULAR	OVERTIME	TOTAL	FEDERAL INCOME TAX	FICA	MEDICARE	OTHER	TOTAL DEDUCTIONS	AMOUNT
1	Baker, Andrea	S	1	800 00		800 00	87 00	49 60	11 60		148 20	651 80
2	Craig, Sommer	S	1	800 00		800 00	87 00	49 60	11 60		148 20	651 80
3	Lewis, Season	S	0	200 00		200 00	14 00	12 40	2 90		29 30	170 70
	Totals			1800 00		1800 00	188 00	111 60	26 10		325 70	1474 30

10 Individual Items: Total Points – 5

Payroll Tax Summary Sheet March 15, 20–   *Memo #5*

	Debit	Credit
Payroll Taxes Expense	$204.00	
FICA Tax Payable		99.20
Medicare Tax Payable		23.20
Unemployment Tax Payable – Federal		12.80
Unemployment Tax Payable – State		68.80

Payroll Tax Summary Sheet March 31, 20–   *Memo #12*

	Debit	Credit
Payroll Taxes Expense	$229.50	
FICA Tax Payable		111.60
Medicare Tax Payable		26.10
Unemployment Tax Payable – Federal		14.40
Unemployment Tax Payable – State		77.40

Worksheet on following page:

125 Individual Items: Total Points – 62.5

Larson's Tours
Worksheet
For the Month Ended March 31, 20—

ACCT. NO.	ACCOUNT NAME	TRIAL BALANCE DEBIT	TRIAL BALANCE CREDIT	ADJUSTMENTS DEBIT	ADJUSTMENTS CREDIT	INCOME STATEMENT DEBIT	INCOME STATEMENT CREDIT	BALANCE SHEET DEBIT	BALANCE SHEET CREDIT
110	Cash	14350 50						14350 50	
120	Petty Cash	300 00						300 00	
130	Supplies	3685 00			(a)2505 00			1180 00	
140	Prepaid Insurance	5140 00			(b)3110 00			2030 00	
150	Automobile	17950 00						17950 00	
160	Office Equipment	2695 00						2695 00	
210	A to Z Office Supply		445 00						445 00
220	Employee Income Tax Pay.		362 00						362 00
230	FICA Tax Payable		421 60						421 60
240	First City Bank		9800 00						9800 00
250	Medicare Tax Payable		98 60						98 60
260	Unempl. Tax Payable – Fed.		27 20						27 20
270	Unempl. Tax Payable – State		146 20						146 20
310	Olive Larson, Capital		23500 00						23500 00
320	Olive Larson, Drawing	2550 00						2550 00	
410	Tour Fees		21905 00				21905 00		
510	Advertising Expense	1118 50				1118 50			
520	Automobile Expense	725 35				725 35			
530	Insurance Expense			(b)3110 00		3110 00			
540	Miscellaneous Expense	1715 75				1715 75			
550	Payroll Taxes Expense	433 50				433 50			
560	Rent Expense	1250 00				1250 00			
570	Salary Expense	3400 00				3400 00			
580	Supplies Expense			(a)2505 00		2505 00			
590	Utilities Expense	1392 00				1392 00			
	Totals	56705 60	56705 60	5615 00	5615 00	15650 10	21905 00	41055 50	34800 60
	Net Income					6254 90			6254 90
						21905 00	21905 00	41055 50	41055 50

32 Individual Items: Total Points – 16

Larson's Tours				
Income Statement				
For the Month Ended March 31, 20—				
Revenue:				
Tour Fees			21905	00
Expenses:				
Advertising Expense	1118	50		
Automobile Expense	725	35		
Insurance Expense	3110	00		
Miscellaneous Expense	1715	75		
Payroll Taxes Expense	433	50		
Rent Expense	1250	00		
Salary Expense	3400	00		
Supplies Expense	2505	00		
Utilities Expense	1392	00		
Total Expenses			15650	10
Net Income			6254	90

21 Individual Items: Total Points – 10.5

Larson's Tours				
Statement of Owner's Equity				
For the Month Ended March 31, 20—				
Capital, March 1, 20—			22000	00
Add: Additional Investment	1500	00		
Net Income	6254	90		
Net Increase in Capital			7754	90
Total			29754	90
Less: Withdrawals			2550	00
Olive Larson, Capital, March 31, 20—			27204	90

47 Individual Items: Total Points – 23.5

Larson's Tours				
Balance Sheet				
March 31, 20—				
Assets				
Cash	14350	50		
Petty Cash	300	00		
Supplies	1180	00		
Prepaid Insurance	2030	00		
Automobile	17950	00		
Office Equipment	2695	00		
Total Assets			38505	50
Liabilities				
A to Z Office Supply	445	00		
Employee Income Tax Payable	362	00		
FICA Tax Payable	421	60		
First City Bank	9800	00		
Medicare Tax Payable	98	60		
Unemployment Tax Payable – Federal	27	20		
Unemployment Tax Payable – State	146	20		
Total Liabilities			11300	60
Owner's Equity				
Olive Larson, Capital			27204	90
Total Liabilities and Owner's Equity			38505	50

50 Individual Items: Total Points – 25

ACCOUNT TITLE	ACCT. NO.	DEBIT		CREDIT	
	Larson's Tours				
	Post-Closing Trial Balance				
	March 31, 20—				
Cash	110	14350	50		
Petty Cash	120	300	00		
Supplies	130	1180	00		
Prepaid Insurance	140	2030	00		
Automobile	150	17950	00		
Office Equipment	160	2695	00		
A to Z Office Supply	210			445	00
Employee Income Tax Payable	220			362	00
FICA Tax Payable	230			421	60
First City Bank	240			9800	00
Medicare Tax Payable	250			98	60
Unemployment Tax Payable – Federal	260			27	20
Unemployment Tax Payable – State	270			146	20
Olive Larson, Capital	310			27204	90
Totals		38505	50	38505	50

Journal	269.0 points
Ledger	264.0 points
Payroll Registers/Payroll Tax Summaries	43.5 points
Worksheet	62.5 points
Financial Statements	75.0 points
Total Points	714.0 points

SELF TEST KEYS

SELF TEST 1

1.01 g

1.02 d

1.03 e

1.04 c

1.05 h

1.06 f

1.07 b

1.08 i

1.09 a

1.010 A bookkeeper's responsibility is to record daily business transactions. An accountant interprets the data recorded by the bookkeeper.

1.011 Any three of the following, any order:

    a. Accounting clerk

    b. Bookkeeper

    c. Accountant or

        General office clerk

SELF TEST 2

2.01 Any five of the following, any order:

    a. Capital (start-up & working capital)

    b. Legal status

    c. Transferability of ownership

    d. Owner's liability for debts

    e. Ease of organization or

       Ease of dissolution,

       Governmental regulations,

       Continuity of ownership

2.02 P

2.03 P

2.04 S

2.05 S

2.06 C

2.07 P

2.08 S

2.09 C

2.010 C

2.011 S

2.012 S

2.013 S

2.014 S

2.015 C

2.016 P

2.017 S

2.018 C

2.019 C

2.020 C

2.021 P

SELF TEST 3

3.01	c	3.018	true
3.02	g	3.019	true
3.03	o	3.020	false
3.04	h	3.021	true
3.05	f	3.022	true
3.06	d	3.023	false
3.07	a	3.024	false
3.08	b		

3.025 a. What accounts are affected?
       b. What are the account classifications?
       c. How are the account balances affected?

3.026 Any order:
       a. Cash paid for daily expenses to produce revenue.
       b. Cash paid to settle the debts of the business.
       c. Cash paid to the owner as a withdrawal for personal use.

3.09 i
3.010 l
3.011 m
3.012 e
3.013 n
3.014 true
3.015 false
3.016 false
3.017 false

SELF TEST 4

4.01
a. asset
b. liability
c. asset
d. liability
e. asset
f. liability
g. capital
h. liability
i. asset
j. capital
k. asset
l. liability
m. asset
n. liability
o. capital

4.02
a. $18,000 = $12,000 + *$6,000*
b. $28,000 = *$14,000* + $14,000
c. *$68,000* = $22,000 + $46,000
d. $6,000 = $3,200 + *$2,800*
e. $27,000 = *$25,100* + $1,900
f. *$4,600* = $2,300 + $2,300

	Accounts Affected	*Account Classification*	*Change in Balance*
	Either order:		
4.03 1.	Cash	Asset	Increase
	Capital	Capital	Increase
2.	Supplies	Asset	Increase
	Cash	Asset	Decrease
3.	Prepaid Ins.	Asset	Increase
	Cash	Asset	Decrease
4.	Supplies	Asset	Increase
	Accts. Payable	Liability	Increase
5.	Accts. Payable	Liability	Decrease
	Cash	Asset	Decrease
6.	Capital	Capital	Decrease
	Cash	Asset	Decrease

	ASSETS			**= LIABILITIES +**	**CAPITAL**
TRANS NO.	*Cash*	*Supplies*	*Prepaid Insurance*	*Accounts Payable*	*J. Osgood, Capital*
1.	*+3,500*				*+3,500*
2.	*−600*	*+600*			
Balance	*2,900*	*600*			*3,500*
3.	*−550*		*+550*		
Balance	*2,350*	*600*	*550*		*3,500*
4.		*+1,100*		*+1,100*	
Balance	*2,350*	*1,700*	*550*	*1,100*	*3,500*
5.	*−350*			*−350*	
Balance	*2,000*	*1,700*	*550*	*750*	*3,500*
6.	*−100*				*−100*
Balance	*1,900*	*1,700*	*550*	*750*	*3,400*

BALANCE PROOF: Total of Assets: *$4,150* = Liabilities + Capital: *$4,150*

SELF TEST 1

1.01	account	1.016	false
1.02	capital	1.017	false
1.03	equities	1.018	true
1.04	liquidity	1.019	false
1.05	chart of accounts	1.020	true
1.06	g		
1.07	i		
1.08	a		
1.09	b		
1.010	k		
1.011	j		
1.012	f		
1.013	d		
1.014	e		
1.015	h		

SELF TEST 2

Teacher's Note: *One answer (j) is used more than once.*

2.01	j	2.06	c
2.02	i	2.07	e
2.03	k	2.08	d
2.04	b	2.09	f
2.05	a	2.010	j

2.011

Sweet Susan's Candy Store					
Balance Sheet					
February 1, 20–					
Assets			Liabilities		
Cash	1550	00	Accounts Payable	1600	00
Supplies	1725	00			
Prepaid Insurance	675	00	Capital		
Equipment	4500	00	Susan Saccharin, Capital	6850	00
Total Assets	8450	00	Total Liabilities & Capital	8450	00

2.012 3

2.013 4

2.014 1

2.015 2

2.016 5

2.017 5

2.018 2

2.019 3

2.020 1

2.021 4

SELF TEST 3

3.01	T	3.07	5
3.02	capital	3.08	3
3.03	assets, liabilities, capital	3.09	1
3.04	beginning balance sheet	3.010	2
3.05	source document	3.011	4
3.06	liquidity		

3.012

JOURNAL						Page 1	
Date 20—	Account Title and Explanation	Doc No.	Post. Ref.	General Debit		General Credit	
Apr. 1	.Cash		110	1000	00		
	Accounts Receivable		120	600	00		
	Supplies		130	2000	00		
	Prepaid Insurance		140	500	00		
	Accounts Payable		210			1800	00
	Joe Haines, Capital	M1	310			2300	00

3.013

Account Title: *Cash*							Account No. *110*		
Date 20—		Explanation	Post. Ref.	Debit		Credit		Balance	
								Debit	Credit
Apr.	1	Opening entry	J1	1000	00			1000	00		

SELF TEST 3 (cont'd)

3.013 (cont'd)

Account Title: *Accounts Receivable*							Account No. 120	
Date 20—		Explanation	Post. Ref.	Debit	Credit	Balance		
						Debit	Credit	
Apr.	1	Opening entry	J1	600 00		600 00		

Account Title: *Supplies*							Account No. 130	
Date 20—		Explanation	Post. Ref.	Debit	Credit	Balance		
						Debit	Credit	
Apr.	1	Opening entry	J1	2000 00		2000 00		

Account Title: *Prepaid Insurance*							Account No. 140	
Date 20—		Explanation	Post. Ref.	Debit	Credit	Balance		
						Debit	Credit	
Apr.	1	Opening entry	J1	500 00		500 00		

Account Title: *Accounts Payable*							Account No. 210	
Date 20—		Explanation	Post. Ref.	Debit	Credit	Balance		
						Debit	Credit	
Apr.	1	Opening entry	J1		1800 00		1800 00	

Account Title: *Joe Haines, Capital*							Account No. 310	
Date 20—		Explanation	Post. Ref.	Debit	Credit	Balance		
						Debit	Credit	
Apr.	1	Opening entry	J1		2300 00		2300 00	

NO SELF TEST 4

SELF TEST 1

1.01	e		1.027	Debit
1.02	d		1.028	Credit
1.03	i		1.029	Credit
1.04	b		1.030	Debit
1.05	c		1.031	Credit
1.06	f		1.032	Debit
1.07	j		1.033	Credit
1.08	h		1.034	Debit
1.09	a		1.035	Debit
1.010	g		1.036	Credit
1.011	L		1.037	Credit
1.012	C		1.038	Debit
1.013	A		1.039	Credit
1.014	A		1.040	Credit
1.015	L		1.041	Debit
1.016	A		1.042	Debit
1.017	E			
1.018	L			
1.019	R			
1.020	A			
1.021	C			
1.022	A			
1.023	E			
1.024	R			
1.025	A			
1.026	A			

SELF TEST 2

2.01 d   2.06 c

2.02 h   2.07 j

2.03 f   2.08 b

2.04 i   2.09 a

2.05 e   2.010 g

2.011

Date 20—		Account Title and Explanation	Doc No.	Post. Ref.	General Debit		General Credit	
June	*1*	*Cash*			*19000*	*00*		
		William Morse, Capital	*R1*				*19000*	*00*
	2	*Rent Expense*			*1900*	*00*		
		Cash	*Ck1*				*1900*	*00*
	3	*Supplies*			*1200*	*00*		
		Cash	*Ck2*				*1200*	*00*
	4	*Equipment*			*1000*	*00*		
		Webster Train Supply Co.	*P1*				*1000*	*00*
	5	*Prepaid Insurance*			*2600*	*00*		
		Cash	*Ck3*				*2600*	*00*
	5	*Cash*			*2900*	*00*		
		Repair Fees	*T5*				*2900*	*00*
	8	*Webster Train Supply Co.*			*1000*	*00*		
		Cash	*Ck4*				*1000*	*00*
	9	*Repair Expense*			*95*	*00*		
		Cash	*Ck5*				*95*	*00*
	9	*Salary Expense*			*1789*	*00*		
		Cash	*Ck6*				*1789*	*00*
	10	*Supplies*			*1440*	*00*		
		Lionel Train Co.	*P2*				*1440*	*00*
	10	*Advertising Expense*			*175*	*00*		
		Cash	*Ck7*				*175*	*00*
	11	*William Morse, Drawing*			*950*	*00*		
		Cash	*Ck8*				*950*	*00*

2.012

JOURNAL						Page 2	
Date 20—	Account Title and Explanation	Doc No.	Post. Ref.	General Debit		General Credit	
June 12	Supplies			80	00		
	Cash	Ck9				80	00
13	Cash			3950	00		
	Repair Fees	T13				3950	00
13	Supplies			1800	00		
	Webster Train Supply Co.	P3				1800	00
14	Salary Expense			1789	00		
	Cash	Ck10				1789	00
15	Lionel Train Co.			600	00		
	Cash	Ck11				600	00
16	Cash			2190	00		
	Repair Fees	T16				2190	00
20	Prepaid Insurance			1410	00		
	Cash	Ck12				1410	00
22	Advertising Expense			285	00		
	Cash	Ck13				285	00
23	William Morse, Drawing			650	00		
	Cash	Ck14				650	00
30	Salary Expense			1789	00		
	Cash	Ck15				1789	00
30	Utilities Expense			560	00		
	Cash	Ck16				560	00

NO SELF TEST 3

SELF TEST 1

1.01 a. Balance Sheet
      b. Income Statement

1.02 It allows for a running balance of each account to be maintained at all times.

1.03 Account: a device use to summarize all the changes that affect a single item in the accounting equation.

1.04 General ledger: a book that contains all of the accounts needed to prepare the financial reports of a business entity.

1.05 Chart of accounts: a list of all the accounts used by a business entity.

1.06 File maintenance: the procedure of arranging accounts in a general ledger, inserting and deleting accounts, and keeping records current.

1.07
a. Assets	110–199
b. Liabilities	210–299
c. Capital	310–399
d. Revenue	410–499
e. Expenses	510–599

1.08
a. Cash	110
b. Supplies	120
c. Accounts Payable	210
d. Jennie Johnson, Capital	310
e. Sales	410
f. Advertising Expense	510
g. Miscellaneous Expense	520

SELF TEST 2

2.01   e

2.02   i

2.03   g

2.04   d

2.05   c

2.06   h

2.07   f

2.08   b

2.09   j

2.010   m

2.011   l

2.012   a

2.013   2

2.014   4

2.015   5

2.016   1

2.017   3

	Balance Side	Increase Side	Decrease Side
2.018	debit	debit	credit
2.019	credit	credit	debit
2.020	credit	credit	debit
2.021	credit	credit	debit
2.022	debit	debit	credit

2.023 h

2.024 a

2.025 c

2.026 b

2.027 e

2.028 d

2.029 f

2.030 g

SELF TEST 3

3.01	f	3.08	j
3.02	a	3.09	h
3.03	g	3.010	k
3.04	b	3.011	d
3.05	c	3.012	e
3.06	i	3.013	n
3.07	m		

3.014 AN ACCOUNT WITH A NORMAL DEBIT BALANCE:

Date 20—		Explanation	Post. Ref.	Debit		Credit		Balance Debit		Credit	
Jan.	1		1	19800	00			19800	00		
	3		1			800	00	19000	00		
	7		1	1250	00			20250	00		
	12		1			1565	00	18685	00		
	18		1			2225	00	16460	00		
	28		1	1458	00			17918	00		
	30		1			3568	00	14350	00		

3.015 AN ACCOUNT WITH A NORMAL CREDIT BALANCE:

Date 20—		Explanation	Post. Ref.	Debit		Credit		Balance Debit		Credit	
Jan.	1		1			11800	00			11800	00
	5		1			800	00			12600	00
	7		1	1687	00					10913	00
	12		1			56	00			10969	00
	18		1	8250	00					2719	00
	28		1	458	00					2261	00
	30		1			5368	00			7629	00

3.016

Account Title		Account Number	Balance Side	Balance Sheet or Income Statement
Cash	a.	110	debit	Balance Sheet
Accounts Payable	b.	210	credit	Balance Sheet
Advertising Expense	c.	510	debit	Income Statement
Sales	d.	410	credit	Income Statement
Petty Cash	e.	120	debit	Balance Sheet
Rent Expense	f.	530	debit	Income Statement
Accounts Receivable	g.	130	debit	Balance Sheet
Miscellaneous Expense	h.	520	debit	Income Statement
Delivery Equipment	i.	170	debit	Balance Sheet
Salary Expense	j.	540	debit	Income Statement
Buildings	k.	160	debit	Balance Sheet
Prepaid Insurance	l.	150	debit	Balance Sheet
Utilities Expense	m.	560	debit	Income Statement
John Smith, Capital	n.	310	credit	Balance Sheet
Supplies	o.	140	debit	Balance Sheet
Supplies Expense	p.	550	debit	Income Statement

3.017   a. 5

b. 3

c. 2

d. 4

e. 1

NO SELF TEST 4

SELF TEST 1

1.01 the length of the accounting cycle for which a business summarizes and reports financial information

1.02 annual; because it corresponds to most federal and state tax reports which are required annually.

1.03 a month, a quarter, or six months

1.04
  a. to prove the equality of the ledger debits and credits

  b. to show the effects of adjustments on accounts

  c. to sort account balances for income statement and balance sheet preparation

  d. to help calculate net income or net loss

1.05 because it is prepared solely for the benefit of the accountant and is not part of the permanent records of the business

1.06
  a. the Heading

  b. the Account Number and Account Title section

  c. the Trial Balance section

  d. the Income Statement section

  e. the Balance Sheet section

1.07
  a. Who – the name of the business

  b. What – the name of the report

  c. When – the date of the report

1.08 the same order as the ledger: assets, liabilities, capital, revenue and expenses

1.09 the chart of accounts

1.010 it increases the owner's equity (capital)

1.011 as a credit entry

1.012 to show that the work above is complete and the columns are to be added

1.013 it decreases the owner's equity (capital)

1.014 as a debit entry

1.015 it indicates that the balances are equal and correct

1.016 the Balance Sheet section

1.017 the Income Statement section

SELF TEST 2

2.01   i

2.02   m

2.03   f

2.04   l

2.05   d

2.06   e

2.07   g

2.08   h

2.09   c

2.010   b

2.011   j

2.012   k

2.013   a

2.014   a. to prove the equality of the ledger debits and credits

   b. to show the effects of adjustments on accounts

   c. to sort account balances for income statement and balance sheet preparation

   d. to help calculate net income or net loss

2.015   because they are the permanent and official records of a business

(Continued next page)

NO SELF TEST 3

Worksheet for Self Test Exercise 2.016

Lawson's Lawn Service
Worksheet
For the Month Ended July 31, 20—

ACCOUNT NAME	TRIAL BALANCE DEBIT	TRIAL BALANCE CREDIT	ADJUSTMENTS DEBIT	ADJUSTMENTS CREDIT	INCOME STATEMENT DEBIT	INCOME STATEMENT CREDIT	BALANCE SHEET DEBIT	BALANCE SHEET CREDIT
Cash	7822 00						7822 00	
Petty Cash	300 00						300 00	
Supplies	4319 00			(a)1008 00			3311 00	
Prepaid Insurance	1600 00			(b) 150 00			1450 00	
John's Garage		1630 00						1630 00
Wick Supplies		300 00						300 00
Durwood Lawson, Capital		9000 00						9000 00
Durwood Lawson, Drawing	500 00						500 00	
Sales		4367 00				4367 00		
Advertising Expense	86 00				86 00			
Insurance Expense			(b) 150 00		150 00			
Miscellaneous Expense	95 00				95 00			
Rent Expense	450 00				450 00			
Supplies Expense			(a)1008 00		1008 00			
Utilities Expense	125 00				125 00			
Totals	15297 00	15297 00	1158 00	1158 00	1914 00	4367 00	13383 00	10930 00
Net Income					2453 00			2453 00
					4367 00	4367 00	13383 00	13383 00

SELF TEST 1

	Net Income	Net Loss
1.01	$ 500.00	
1.02	4,000.00	
1.03	1,575.00	
1.04		150.00
1.05	4,620.00	
1.06		400.00
1.07	7,785.00	
1.08	2,771.00	

Teacher's Note: Each item in the form below counts as **one point**, *including each line of the heading. All account titles, amounts and rulings count as single items.* **Total Points – 24**

1.09

Fox Amusement Park				
Income Statement				
For the Month Ended October 31, 20—				
Revenue:				
Admissions Income	11500	00		
Concessions Income	2600	00		
Total Revenue			14100	00
Expenses:				
Advertising Expense	2500	00		
Rent Expense	3500	00		
Utilities Expense	780	00		
Total Expenses			6780	00
Net Income			7320	00

SELF TEST 1 (cont'd)

Teacher's Note: Each item in the form below counts as **one point**, *including each line of the heading. All account titles, amounts and rulings count as single items.* **Total Points – 24**

1.010

Lawrence Landscaping					
Income Statement					
For the Month Ended January 31, 20—					
Revenue:					
Sales				28500	00
Expenses:					
Advertising Expense	9950	00			
Miscellaneous Expense	165	00			
Rent Expense	12000	00			
Salary Expense	6000	00			
Utilities Expense	1500	00			
Total Expenses				29615	00
Net Loss				1115	00

SELF TEST 2

	Total Assets	Total Liabilities	Total Capital	Total Drawing	Net Income or (Net Loss)	Ending Capital Balance
2.01	$ 3,158.00	$1,228.00	$1,580.00	$ 800.00	$1,150.00	*1930.00*
		3158.00 =	1228.00	+	1930.00	
2.02	6,659.00	2,860.00	3,990.00	1,680.00	1,489.00	*3799.00*
		6659.00 =	2860.00	+	3799.00	
2.03	4,527.00	1,755.00	1,987.00	200.00	985.00	*2772.00*
		4527.00 =	1755.00	+	2772.00	
2.04	2,094.00	1,575.00	1,199.00	500.00	(180.00)	*519.00*
		2094.00 =	1575.00	+	519.00	
2.05	11,335.00	3,270.00	7,000.00	195.00	1,260.00	*8065.00*
		11335.00 =	3270.00	+	8065.00	
2.06	7,759.00	5,250.00	3,690.00	895.00	(286.00)	*2509.00*
		7759.00 =	5250.00	+	2509.00	
2.07	7,790.00	2,610.00	3,960.00	220.00	1,440.00	*5180.00*
		7790.00 =	2610.00	+	5180.00	
2.08	18,540.00	9,880.00	7,890.00	1,200.00	1,970.00	*8660.00*
		18540.00 =	9880.00	+	8660.00	

2.09

Teacher's Note: *Each item in the form below counts as* **one point**, *including each line of the heading. All account titles, amounts and rulings count as single items.* **Total Points – 27**

Johnson's Computer Service				
Income Statement				
For the Month Ended December 31, 20—				
Revenue:				
Computer Sales	11500	00		
Repairs Income	11500	00		
Total Revenue			23000	00
Expenses:				
Advertising Expense	12500	00		
Miscellaneous Expense	1200	00		
Rent Expense	9600	00		
Utilities Expense	1780	00		
Total Expenses			25080	00
Net Loss			2080	00

2.010

Teacher's Note: *Each item in the form below counts as* **one point**, *including each line of the heading. All account titles, amounts and rulings count as single items.* **Total Points – 16**

Johnson's Computer Service				
Statement of Owner's Equity				
For the Month Ended December 31, 20—				
Capital, December 1, 20—			19200	00
Less: Net Loss	2080	00		
Withdrawals	1900	00		
Net Decrease in Capital			3980	00
Kellie Johnson, Capital, December 31, 20—			15220	00

SELF TEST 3

3.01   a   3.06   e

3.02   f   3.07   g

3.03   b   3.08   c

3.04   j   3.09   d

3.05   h

3.010   **Teacher's Note:** *Each item in the form below counts as* **one point***, including each line of the heading. All account titles, amounts and rulings count as single items.*
Total Points – 26

Miller Company				
Income Statement				
For the Month Ended April 30, 20—				
Revenue:				
Sales			1900	00
Expenses:				
Advertising Expense	50	00		
Insurance Expense	110	00		
Miscellaneous Expense	75	00		
Rent Expense	450	00		
Repair Expense	95	00		
Utilities Expense	285	00		
Total Expenses			1065	00
Net Income			835	00

SELF TEST 3 (cont'd)

3.011   **Teacher's Note:** *Each item in the form below counts as* **one point**, *including each line of the heading. All account titles, amounts and rulings count as single items.*
Total Points – 16

Floor-Shine Company				
Statement of Owner's Equity				
For the Month Ended November 30, 20—				
Capital, November 1, 20—			8000	00
Add: Net Income			178	00
Total			8178	00
Less: Withdrawals			560	00
Mike Ford, Capital, December 31, 20—			7618	00

3.012   **Teacher's Note:** *Each item in the form below counts as* **one point**, *including each line of the heading. All account titles, amounts, rulings and blank divider lines after double rulings count as single items.* **Total Points – 31**

Floor-Shine Company				
Balance Sheet				
November 30, 20—				
Assets				
Cash	5844	00		
Petty Cash	300	00		
Supplies	1300	00		
Prepaid Insurance	400	00		
Total Assets			7844	00
Liabilities				
Tyson Office Supply	166	00		
Office Systems, Inc.	60	00		
Total Liabilities			226	00
Owner's Equity				
Mike Ford, Capital			7618	00
Total Liabilities and Owner's Equity			7844	00

NO SELF TEST 4

SELF TEST 1

1.01	f		1.07	k
1.02	i		1.08	b
1.03	d		1.09	j
1.04	e		1.010	a
1.05	g		1.011	h
1.06	c			

1.012   **Teacher's Note:** *Each item in the journal entry below counts **two** points, including the year, the month and the day of the month. All headings, amounts, account titles and account numbers count as single items. This problem has 17 individual items.*
Total Points – 34

JOURNAL							Page 5	
Date 20—		Account Title and Explanation	Doc No.	Post. Ref.	General Debit		General Credit	
		Adjusting Entries						
Nov.	*30*	*Supplies Expense*		560	600	00		
		Supplies		130			600	00
	30	*Insurance Expense*		520	400	00		
		Prepaid Insurance		140			400	00

SELF TEST 1 (cont'd)

1.013   ***Teacher's Note:*** *Each item in the ledger accounts below counts* ***two*** *points, including the year, the month and the day of the month. All amounts and posting reference numbers count as single items. This problem has 20 individual items.* ***Total Points – 40***

Account Title: *Supplies*   Account No. *130*

Date 20—		Explanation	Post. Ref.	Debit		Credit		Balance Debit		Balance Credit	
Nov.	1		✔					1900	00		
	30		J5			600	00	1300	00		

Account Title: *Prepaid Insurance*   Account No. *140*

Date 20—		Explanation	Post. Ref.	Debit		Credit		Balance Debit		Balance Credit	
Nov.	1		✔					800	00		
	30		J5			400	00	400	00		

Account Title: *Insurance Expense*   Account No. *520*

Date 20—		Explanation	Post. Ref.	Debit		Credit		Balance Debit		Balance Credit	
Nov.	30		J5	400	00			400	00		

Account Title: *Supplies Expense*   Account No. *560*

Date 20—		Explanation	Post. Ref.	Debit		Credit		Balance Debit		Balance Credit	
Nov.	30		J5	600	00			600	00		

SELF TEST 2

2.01 Suggested answer:
to prepare temporary accounts for a new fiscal period and to transfer net income or net loss to the owner's capital account.

2.02 Any order:
a. revenue accounts
b. expense accounts
c. Income Summary
d. the owner's drawing account

2.03 Suggested answers:
a. close revenue into Income Summary
b. close expenses into Income Summary
c. close Income Summary into Capital
d. close Drawing into Capital

2.04 Debit: Sales
Credit: Income Summary

2.05 Debit: Income Summary
Credit: Advertising Expense

2.06 Debit: Income Summary
Credit: Capital

2.07 Debit: Capital
Credit: Income Summary

2.08 Debit: Capital
Credit: Drawing

2.09 Suggested answer:
Accounts whose balances carry forward from one fiscal period to the next.

SELF TEST 2 (cont'd)

2.010   **Teacher's Note:** *Each item in the journal below counts for **one** point, including the page number, the year, the month and the day of the month. All amounts, account titles and account numbers count as single items. This problem has 45 individual items.*
Total Points – 45

JOURNAL									Page *1*
Date 20—		Account Title and Explanation	Doc No.	Post. Ref.	General Debit			General Credit	
		Adjusting Entries							
July	*31*	*Supplies Expense*			*1008*	*00*			
		Supplies						*1008*	*00*
	31	*Insurance Expense*			*150*	*00*			
		Prepaid Insurance						*150*	*00*
		Closing Entries							
	31	*Sales*			*4367*	*00*			
		Income Summary						*4367*	*00*
	31	*Income Summary*			*1914*	*00*			
		Advertising Expense						*86*	*00*
		Insurance Expense						*150*	*00*
		Miscellaneous Expense						*95*	*00*
		Rent Expense						*450*	*00*
		Supplies Expense						*1008*	*00*
		Utilities Expense						*125*	*00*
	31	*Income Summary*			*2453*	*00*			
		Durwood Lawson, Capital						*2453*	*00*
	31	*Durwood Lawson, Capital*			*500*	*00*			
		Durwood Lawson, Drawing						*500*	*00*

SELF TEST 3

3.01	f	3.010	a
3.02	h	3.011	i
3.03	k	3.012	n
3.04	d	3.013	j
3.05	g	3.014	4
3.06	m		3
3.07	b		5
3.08	c		1
3.09	e		2

3.015

Account Title	Account adjusted from adjusting entries?		Account closed during closing procedure?		Account appears on the Post-Closing Trial Balance?	
	YES	NO	YES	NO	YES	NO
Cash		X		X	X	
Utilities Expense		X	X			X
Office Max (Liability)		X		X	X	
Advertising Expense		X	X			X
Petty Cash		X		X	X	
Commission Income		X	X			X
John Jones, Capital		X		X	X	
Insurance Expense	X		X			X
Supplies	X			X	X	
Supplies Expense	X		X			X
Prepaid Insurance	X			X	X	
John Jones, Drawing		X	X			X
Rent Expense		X	X			X
NBT Bank (Liability)		X		X	X	
Income Summary		X	X			X
Sales Revenue		X	X			X
Misc. Expense		X	X			X
Equipment		X		X	X	
Law Library		X		X	X	

NO SELF TEST 4

SELF TEST 1

Teacher's Note: Each answer is worth 5 points. **Total Points – 100**

1.01 Suggested answers:
   a. accounting for withholding from employees' wages
   b. accounting for employer payroll taxes
   c. accounting for employee benefits programs

1.02 Suggested answers:
   a. hiring employees
   b. timekeeping
   c. preparing and paying the payroll

1.03 a. Social Security (FICA) taxes
   b. federal income taxes
   c. state income taxes

1.04 Form W-4

1.05 Any order:
   a. marital status
   b. number of dependents

1.06 $76,200.00

1.07 Any order:
   a. retirement
   b. survivor's benefits
   c. disability
   d. Medicare

1.08 the first $7,000.00 earned by an employee

1.09 voluntary deductions

1.010 Suggested answer:
   Both the employer and the employee contribute equally.

SELF TEST 2

Teacher's Note: Each answer is worth 2 points. **Total Points – 38**

2.01	j		2.011	f
2.02	d		2.012	T
2.03	k		2.013	F
2.04	l		2.014	T
2.05	e		2.015	F
2.06	a		2.016	T
2.07	g		2.017	T
2.08	b		2.018	F
2.09	c		2.019	F
2.010	i			

2.020   *Teacher's Note:* Each answer is worth 4 points. **Total Points – 68**

Employee _Katherine Ludwig_
Employee # _22_
Period Ending _October 30, 20—_

ABC Company

DATE	MORNING		AFTERNOON		OVERTIME		HOURS	
	IN	OUT	IN	OUT	IN	OUT	REG	OT
10/26	7:55	12:04	1:05	5:03			8	0
10/27	8:01	12:00	12:55	5:01	5:33	9:00	8	3.5
10/28	8:00	11:59	12:59	5:00			8	0
10/29	7:56	11:58	1:01	5:03			8	0
10/30	7:55	12:03	12:58	5:02	6:00	8:30	8	2.5

	HOURS	RATE	AMOUNT
REGULAR	40.0	8.75	350.00
OVERTIME	6.0	13.125	78.75
TOTAL HOURS	46	TOTAL EARNINGS	428.75

Supervisor's OT Approval _Joe Jensen_

Employee's Signature _Katherine Ludwig_

SELF TEST 3

3.01 **Teacher's Note:** *Each answer is worth 1 point.* **Total Points – 54**

Employee No. 6							
Name *Harrison Ford*							
Period Ending *January 15, 20—*							
Morning		Afternoon		Overtime		Hours	
IN	OUT	IN	OUT	IN	OUT	REG	OT
7:59	12:01	1:00	5:02			8	0
8:03	11:59	1:01	5:03			8	0
8:00	12:00	1:02	5:00			8	0
7:56	11:57	1:01	5:03	6:00	8:00	8	2
7:59	12:03	1:00	5:00			8	0
8:01	12:00	1:03	5:00			8	0
7:56	11:58	1:00	5:04	6:30	7:30	8	1
8:00	12:00	1:01	5:01			8	0
7:58	11:57	1:05	5:06	6:00	8:45	8	2.75
7:59	12:04	1:00	5:01			8	0

	HOURS	RATE	AMOUNT
REGULAR	80.0	9.50	760.00
OVERTIME	5.75	14.25	81.94
TOTAL	85.75		841.94

Employee No. 8							
Name *Mike Black*							
Period Ending *January 15, 20—*							
Morning		Afternoon		Overtime		Hours	
IN	OUT	IN	OUT	IN	OUT	REG	OT
7:59	12:01	1:00	5:02			8	0
8:03	11:59	1:01	4:03			7	0
9:00	12:00	1:02	5:00			7	0
7:56	11:57	1:01	5:03	6:00	8:00	8	2
7:59	12:03	1:00	5:00			8	0
8:01	12:00	1:03	5:00			8	0
7:56	11:58	1:00	5:04	5:30	7:30	8	2
9:00	12:00	1:01	5:01			7	0
7:58	11:57	1:05	5:06			8	0
7:59	12:04	1:00	3:01			6	0

	HOURS	RATE	AMOUNT
REGULAR	75.0	7.40	555.00
OVERTIME	4.0	11.10	44.40
TOTAL	79.0		599.40

SELF TEST 3 (cont'd)

3.01   *Teacher's Note: Each answer is worth 1 point.* **Total Points – 83**

PAYROLL REGISTER for the Semimonthly Payroll Period Ended June 15, 20—

NO.	NAME	MARITAL STATUS	EXEMP.	EARNINGS REGULAR	EARNINGS OVERTIME	EARNINGS TOTAL	DEDUCTIONS FEDERAL INCOME TAX	DEDUCTIONS FICA	DEDUCTIONS STATE INCOME TAX	DEDUCTIONS HEALTH INSURANCE	DEDUCTIONS TOTAL DEDUCTIONS	NET PAY AMOUNT
1	Abbott, Patricia	M	2	522 00	14 80	536 80	4 00	41 07	12 54	30 00	87 61	449 19
5	Adams, Chris	S	1	582 00	22 80	604 80	57 00	46 27	20 30		123 57	481 23
3	Banks, Wilma	M	3	645 00	28 30	673 30	8 00	51 51	13 18	38 00	110 69	562 61
6	French, Donna	M	2	370 00		370 00	0 00	28 31	5 48	30 00	63 79	306 21
2	Griffith, Mindy	M	4	692 00	38 00	730 00	0 00	55 85	10 46		66 31	663 69
4	Harris, James	S	0	696 00	32 00	728 00	93 00	55 69	30 74		179 43	548 57
7	James, Tom	M	1	680 00		680 00	46 00	52 02	23 66	30 00	151 68	528 32
12	Martin, Mary	M	2	708 00	12 00	720 00	34 00	55 08	20 27	30 00	139 35	580 65
11	Northrop, Greg	S	1	687 00		687 00	69 00	52 56	23 66	28 00	173 22	513 78
10	Patton, Harry	M	3	568 00	11 00	579 00	0 00	44 29	9 15	44 00	97 44	481 56
8	Trent, Joe	S	1	592 00		592 00	54 00	45 29	19 96	28 00	147 25	444 75
9	Watson, Joanne	S	2	472 00		472 00	20 00	36 11	9 85	28 00	93 96	378 04
	Totals			7214 00	158 90	7372 90	385 00	564 05	199 25	286 00	1434 30	5938 60

NO SELF TEST 4

SELF TEST 1

1.01 i

1.02 b

1.03 j

1.04 h

1.05 g

1.06 e

1.07 c

1.08 d

1.09 a

1.010 Suggested answers:

    a. salary or wage amounts paid

    b. amounts deducted from employees' earnings

    c. expenses involved with the payroll

    d. payroll taxes paid to the government by the employees and employer

1.011 Suggested answer:

Until the funds are paid to the government, they are amounts *owed*, thus becoming a liability.

Suggested answers:

1.012 a. total wages/salaries for the pay period

    b. Salary Expense

    c. debit Salary Expense for $2,730.00

1.013 a. total income tax withheld from employees' wages for the pay period

    b. Employee Income Tax Payable

    c. credit Employee Income Tax Payable for $231.00

1.014 a. amount withheld from employees' wages for FICA tax for the pay period

    b. FICA Tax Payable

    c. credit FICA Tax Payable for $169.26

1.015 a. total Medicare Tax deducted from employees' wages for the pay period

    b. Medicare Tax Payable

    c. credit Medicare Tax Payable for $39.59

1.016 a. the total of all employees' net pay *or* the amount of the check written to the payroll account

    b. Cash

    c. credit cash for $2,290.15

SELF TEST 2

2.01   b

2.02   l

2.03   j

2.04   h

2.05   g

2.06   f

2.07   e

2.08   i

2.09   d

2.010   a

2.011   c

2.012   Suggested answers:
  a. matching FICA tax
  b. matching Medicate tax
  c. federal unemployment tax
  d. state unemployment tax

2.013   Any order:
  a. Employee Income Tax Payable
  b. FICA Tax Payable
  c. Medicare Tax Payable
  d. Cash

2.014   c

2.015   a

2.016   h

2.017   g

2.018   i

2.019   f

2.020   d

2.021   e

SELF TEST 3

3.01	c	3.014	d
3.02	d	3.015	b
3.03	c	3.016	b
3.04	d	3.017	d
3.05	d	3.018	b
3.06	c		
3.07	b		

3.019 Any order:
    a. matching FICA tax
    b. matching Medicare tax
    c. federal unemployment tax
    d. state unemployment tax

3.020 Any order:
    a. Employee Income Tax Payable
    b. FICA Tax Payable
    c. Medicare Tax Payable
    d. Cash

3.08 c
3.09 b
3.010 b
3.011 b
3.012 b
3.013 b

NO SELF TEST 4

LIFEPAC 10 is a business simulation that represents a complete accounting cycle. To ensure that the student starts and continues correctly, the project should be completed under your supervision. The work must be neat and legible, and corrections should follow the procedures discussed in previous LIFEPACs. Normally, work of this type is done in pen with the exception of the worksheet; however, you may feel that using a pencil is a better way to complete this project. NOTE: Students may use previous LIFEPACs for reference while completing this simulation.

There are no Self Tests for this LIFEPAC.

TEST

KEYS

LIFEPAC TEST 1

Teacher's Note: Each answer is worth 1 point. **Total Points – 30**

1.	a		16.	c
2.	c		17.	a
3.	b		18.	c
4.	c		19.	c
5.	a		20.	b
6.	b		21.	d
7.	d		22.	b
8.	c		23.	a
9.	a		24.	c
10.	b		25.	d
11.	c		26.	b
12.	d		27.	d
13.	a		28.	b
14.	c		29.	a
15.	a		30.	b

LIFEPAC TEST 1 (cont'd)

Teacher's Note: Each answer is worth 1 point. **Total Points – 104**

TRANS NO.	Cash	Accounts Receivable	Prepaid Insurance	Office Supplies	Accounts Payable	M. Smith, Capital
1.	+6,000					+6,000
2.	–1,500					–1,500
Balance	4,500					4,500
3.	–180					–180
Balance	4,320					4,320
4.	+2,500					+2,500
Balance	6,820					6,820
5.				+260	+260	
Balance	6,820			260	260	6,820
6.		+1,500				+1,500
Balance	6,820	1,500		260	260	8,320
7.	–850					–850
Balance	5,970	1,500		260	260	7,470
8.	–260				–260	
Balance	5,710	1,500		260		7,470
9.	+1,500	–1,500				
Balance	7,210			260		7,470
10.		+1,100				+1,100
Balance	7,210	1,100		260		8,570
11.				+350	+350	
Balance	7,210	1,100		610	350	8,570
12.	+1,100	–1,100				
Balance	8,310			610	350	8,570
13.	–850					–850
Balance	7,460			610	350	7,720
14.	–95					–95
Balance	7,365			610	350	7,625
15.	–385					–385
Balance	6,980			610	350	7,240
16.	–2,400		+2,400			
Balance	4,580		2,400	610	350	7,240
17.	–1,600					–1,600
Balance	2,980		2,400	610	350	5,640

BALANCE PROOF: Total of Assets: _____$5,990_____ = Liabilities + Capital: _____$5,990_____

LIFEPAC TEST 2

PART I

Teacher's Note: Each answer is worth 1 point. **Total Points – 30**

1.	c	16.	a
2.	b	17.	b
3.	a	18.	d
4.	d	19.	b
5.	c	20.	a
6.	a	21.	d
7.	d	22.	d
8.	a	23.	b or c
9.	c	24.	b
10.	a	25.	a
11.	c	26.	a
12.	b	27.	d
13.	d	28.	b
14.	c	29.	c
15.	c	30.	c

PART II

31. **Teacher's Note:** *Every item is worth 1 point. Account titles and account numbers count as separate items. Each line of the 2-line heading counts as a separate item.* **Total Points – 19**

Job-Find *Chart of Accounts*			
Assets		*Liabilities*	
Cash	*110*	*Accounts Payable*	*210*
Office Supplies	*120*	*Notes Payable*	*220*
Prepaid Insurance	*130*		
Office Equipment	*140*	*Capital*	
		Gail Short, Capital	*310*

LIFEPAC TEST 2 (cont'd)

32. **Teacher's Note:** *Each balance sheet item, including each ruling (underline), counts as a single item. Each line of the heading counts as a single item, and column headings, account titles and amounts count as single items.* **Total Points – 31**

<table>
<tr><td colspan="6" align="center">*Job-Find*</td></tr>
<tr><td colspan="6" align="center">*Balance Sheet*</td></tr>
<tr><td colspan="6" align="center">*January 1, 20–*</td></tr>
<tr><td colspan="6"></td></tr>
<tr><td align="center">*Assets*</td><td></td><td></td><td align="center">*Liabilities*</td><td></td><td></td></tr>
<tr><td>*Cash*</td><td>7500</td><td>00</td><td>*Accounts Payable* 3700.00</td><td></td><td></td></tr>
<tr><td>*Office Supplies*</td><td>3675</td><td>00</td><td>*Notes Payable* 2600.00</td><td></td><td></td></tr>
<tr><td>*Prepaid Insurance*</td><td>1125</td><td>00</td><td>*Total Liabilities*</td><td>6300</td><td>00</td></tr>
<tr><td>*Office Equipment*</td><td>6675</td><td>00</td><td></td><td></td><td></td></tr>
<tr><td></td><td></td><td></td><td align="center">*Capital*</td><td></td><td></td></tr>
<tr><td></td><td></td><td></td><td>*Gail Short, Capital*</td><td>12675</td><td>00</td></tr>
<tr><td>*Total Assets*</td><td>18975</td><td>00</td><td>*Total Liabilities & Capital*</td><td>18975</td><td>00</td></tr>
<tr><td></td><td></td><td></td><td></td><td></td><td></td></tr>
</table>

33. **Teacher's Note:** *Each journal item counts for* **one-half** *point, including the page number, the year, the month and the day of the month. All amounts, account titles, document numbers and account numbers count as single items. This journal has 26 individual items.* **Total Points – 13**

<table>
<tr><td colspan="4" align="center">**JOURNAL**</td><td colspan="2" align="right">Page *1*</td></tr>
<tr><td>Date
20—</td><td>Account Title and Explanation</td><td>Doc
No.</td><td>Post.
Ref.</td><td>General
Debit</td><td>General
Credit</td></tr>
<tr><td>*Jan.* 1</td><td>*Cash*</td><td></td><td>*110*</td><td>7500 00</td><td></td></tr>
<tr><td></td><td>*Office Supplies*</td><td></td><td>*120*</td><td>3675 00</td><td></td></tr>
<tr><td></td><td>*Prepaid Insurance*</td><td></td><td>*130*</td><td>1125 00</td><td></td></tr>
<tr><td></td><td>*Office Equipment*</td><td></td><td>*140*</td><td>6675 00</td><td></td></tr>
<tr><td></td><td>*Accounts Payable*</td><td></td><td>*210*</td><td></td><td>3700 00</td></tr>
<tr><td></td><td>*Notes Payable*</td><td></td><td>*220*</td><td></td><td>2600 00</td></tr>
<tr><td></td><td>*Gail Short, Capital*</td><td>*M1*</td><td>*310*</td><td></td><td>12675 00</td></tr>
<tr><td></td><td></td><td></td><td></td><td></td><td></td></tr>
</table>

LIFEPAC TEST 2 (cont'd)

34. ***Teacher's Note:*** *Each ledger account item counts for* **one-half** *point, including the year, month and the day of the month. All account titles, account numbers, explanations, posting reference numbers and amounts count as single items. Each ledger account has 9 individual items (4.5 points) and there are 7 ledger accounts. The total points are rounded up from 31.5.*
Total Points – 32

Account Title: *Cash*   Account No. *110*

Date 20—		Explanation	Post. Ref.	Debit		Credit		Balance			
								Debit		Credit	
Jan.	1	Opening entry	J1	7500	00			7500	00		

Account Title: *Office Supplies*   Account No. *120*

Date 20—		Explanation	Post. Ref.	Debit		Credit		Balance			
								Debit		Credit	
Jan.	1	Opening entry	J1	3675	00			3675	00		

Account Title: *Prepaid Insurance*   Account No. *130*

Date 20—		Explanation	Post. Ref.	Debit		Credit		Balance			
								Debit		Credit	
Jan.	1	Opening entry	J1	1125	00			1125	00		

Account Title: *Office Equipment*   Account No. *140*

Date 20—		Explanation	Post. Ref.	Debit		Credit		Balance			
								Debit		Credit	
Jan.	1	Opening entry	J1	6675	00			6675	00		

LIFEPAC TEST 2 (cont'd)

Account Title: *Accounts Payable* **Account No. 210**

Date 20—		Explanation	Post. Ref.	Debit		Credit		Balance Debit		Credit	
Jan.	1	Opening entry	J1			3700	00			3700	00

Account Title: *Notes Payable* **Account No. 220**

Date 20—		Explanation	Post. Ref.	Debit		Credit		Balance Debit		Credit	
Jan.	1	Opening entry	J1			2600	00			2600	00

Account Title: *Gail Short, Capital* **Account No. 310**

Date 20—		Explanation	Post. Ref.	Debit		Credit		Balance Debit		Credit	
Jan.	1	Opening entry	J1			12675	00			12675	00

LIFEPAC TEST 3

PART I

Teacher's Note: Each answer is worth 1 point. **Total Points – 25**

1.	a		14.	b
2.	b		15.	a
3.	b		16.	c
4.	c		17.	a
5.	c		18.	b
6.	b		19.	a
7.	c		20.	d
8.	a		21.	b
9.	b		22.	a
10.	c		23.	c
11.	a		24.	b
12.	c		25.	c
13.	c			

PART II

26. **Teacher's Note:** *Each item in the T accounts below counts as one point, including the account title, the date and the amount for each entry. This problem has 64 individual items.*
    Total Points – 64

Cash			
(1-1)	1000.00	(1-2)	20.00
(1-3)	115.00	(1-4)	100.00
(1-10)	145.00	(1-6)	10.00
		(1-7)	30.00
		(1-8)	5.00
		(1-9)	15.00
		(1-11)	10.00
		(1-12)	150.00
		(1-13)	70.00

Supplies	
(1-2)	20.00
(1-5)	70.00

Prepaid Insurance	
(1-7)	30.00

26.   (cont'd)

Ross's Supply		
(1-13) 70.00	(1-5) 70.00

Advertising Expense	
(1-11) 10.00	

Sarah Clark, Capital	
	(1-1) 1000.00

Miscellaneous Expense	
(1-8) 5.00	

Sarah Clark, Drawing	
(1-12) 150.00	

Rent Expense	
(1-4) 100.00	

Sales	
	(1-3) 115.00
	(1-10) 145.00

Repair Expense	
(1-6) 10.00	

Utilities Expense	
(1-9) 15.00	

LIFEPAC TEST 3 (cont'd)

PART III

27. **Teacher's Note:** *Each item in the journal below counts as* **one-half** *point, including the page number, the year, the month and the day of the month. All account titles, document numbers and amounts count as single items. This problem has 75 individual items, so the points are rounded up from 37.5.* **Total Points – 38**

JOURNAL							Page *1*	
Date 20—		Account Title and Explanation	Doc No.	Post. Ref.	General Debit		General Credit	
Oct.	1	Cash			7000	00		
		Cody Williams, Capital	R1				7000	00
	2	Supplies			250	00		
		Cash	Ck1				250	00
	3	Rent Expense			700	00		
		Cash	Ck2				700	00
	4	Supplies			900	00		
		Blue Ridge Supply Co.	P1				900	00
	5	Repairs Expense			50	00		
		Cash	Ck3				50	00
	6	Prepaid Insurance			1000	00		
		Cash	Ck4				1000	00
	7	Cash			3500	00		
		Sales	T7				3500	00
	8	Advertising Expense			75	00		
		Cash	Ck5				75	00
	9	Cody Williams, Drawing			250	00		
		Cash	Ck6				250	00
	10	Blue Ridge Supply Co.			450	00		
		Cash	Ck7				450	00
	11	Miscellaneous Expense			32	00		
		Cash	Ck8				32	00
	12	Equipment			3000	00		
		Cash	Ck9				3000	00

LIFEPAC TEST 4

*Teacher's Note: Each item in the journal below counts as **one-half** point, including the page number, the year, the month and the day of the month. All amounts, account titles, document numbers and account numbers count as single items. This problem has 116 individual items.* **Total Points – 58**

Date 20—		Account Title and Explanation	Doc No.	Post. Ref.	General Debit		General Credit	
Apr.	1	Cash		110	68000	00		
		Office Equipment		140	15000	00		
		Robert Burns, Capital	M1	310			83000	00
	2	Land		160	62000	00		
		Building		170	110000	00		
		Mortgage Payable		220			139000	00
		Cash	Ck100	110			33000	00
	3	Office Supplies		130	975	00		
		Accounts Payable	P2	210			975	00
	4	Automobile		150	17500	00		
		Cash	Ck101	110			17500	00
	5	Salaries Expense		530	600	00		
		Cash	Ck102	110			600	00
	6	Cash		110	8900	00		
		Commissions	R1	420			8900	00
	7	Advertising Expense		510	250	00		
		Cash	Ck103	110			250	00
	8	Accounts Payable		210	75	00		
		Cash	Ck104	110			75	00
	9	Office Equipment		140	1840	00		
		Accounts Payable	P3	210			1840	00
	10	Accounts Receivable		120	210	00		
		Appraisal Fees	M2	410			210	00
	11	Salaries Expense		530	640	00		
		Cash	Ck105	110			640	00
	12	Cash		110	210	00		
		Accounts Receivable	R2	120			210	00
	13	Robert Burns, Drawing		320	1500	00		
		Cash	Ck106	110			1500	00

JOURNAL — Page 1

LIFEPAC TEST 4 (cont'd)

*Teacher's Note: Each item in the ledger accounts below counts as **one-half** point, including the account title, account number, year, month, day, posting reference number and correct debit or credit amounts. Points are listed underneath each ledger account.*

Account Title: *Cash* — **Account No. 110**

Date 20—		Explanation	Post. Ref.	Debit		Credit		Balance			
								Debit		Credit	
Apr.	1		J1	68000	00			68000	00		
	2		J1			33000	00	35000	00		
	4		J1			17500	00	17500	00		
	5		J1			600	00	16900	00		
	6		J1	8900	00			25800	00		
	7		J1			250	00	25550	00		
	8		J1			75	00	25475	00		
	11		J1			640	00	24835	00		
	12		J1	210	00			25045	00		
	13		J1			1500	00	23545	00		

Total Points – 22

Account Title: *Accounts Receivable* — **Account No. 120**

Date 20—		Explanation	Post. Ref.	Debit		Credit		Balance			
								Debit		Credit	
Apr.	10		J1	210	00			210	00		
	12		J1			210	00	———			

Total Points – 6

Account Title: *Office Supplies* — **Account No. 130**

Date 20—		Explanation	Post. Ref.	Debit		Credit		Balance			
								Debit		Credit	
Apr.	3		J1	975	00			975	00		

Total Points – 4

Accounting LIFEPAC Test Keys

LIFEPAC TEST 4 (cont'd)

Account Title: *Office Equipment* **Account No. *140***

Date 20—		Explanation	Post. Ref.	Debit		Credit		Balance Debit		Credit	
Apr.	1		J1	15000	00			15000	00		
	9		J1	1840	00			16840	00		

Total Points – 6

Account Title: *Automobile* **Account No. *150***

Date 20—		Explanation	Post. Ref.	Debit		Credit		Balance Debit		Credit	
Apr.	4		J1	17500	00			17500	00		

Total Points – 4

Account Title: *Land* **Account No. *160***

Date 20—		Explanation	Post. Ref.	Debit		Credit		Balance Debit		Credit	
Apr.	2		J1	62000	00			62000	00		

Total Points – 4

Account Title: *Building* **Account No. *170***

Date 20—		Explanation	Post. Ref.	Debit		Credit		Balance Debit		Credit	
Apr.	2		J1	110000	00			110000	00		

Total Points – 4

Account Title: *Accounts Payable* **Account No. *210***

Date 20—		Explanation	Post. Ref.	Debit		Credit		Balance Debit		Credit	
Apr.	3		J1			975	00			975	00
	8		J1	75	00					900	00
	9		J1			1840	00			2740	00

Total Points – 8

256

LIFEPAC TEST 4 (cont'd)

Account Title: *Mortgage Payable*							Account No. *220*			
Date 20—		Explanation	Post. Ref.	Debit		Credit		Balance		
								Debit	Credit	
Apr.	2		J1			139000	00		139000	00

Total Points – 4

Account Title: *Robert Burns, Capital*							Account No. *310*			
Date 20—		Explanation	Post. Ref.	Debit		Credit		Balance		
								Debit	Credit	
Apr.	1		J1			83000	00		83000	00

Total Points – 4

Account Title: *Robert Burns, Drawing*							Account No. *320*			
Date 20—		Explanation	Post. Ref.	Debit		Credit		Balance		
								Debit	Credit	
Apr.	13		J1	1500	00			1500	00	

Total Points – 4

Account Title: *Appraisal Fees*							Account No. *410*			
Date 20—		Explanation	Post. Ref.	Debit		Credit		Balance		
								Debit	Credit	
Apr.	10		J1			210	00		210	00

Total Points – 4

Account Title: *Commissions*							Account No. *420*			
Date 20—		Explanation	Post. Ref.	Debit		Credit		Balance		
								Debit	Credit	
Apr.	6		J1			8900	00		8900	00

Total Points – 4

LIFEPAC TEST 4 (cont'd)

Account Title: *Advertising Expense*   **Account No.** *510*

Date 20—		Explanation	Post. Ref.	Debit		Credit		Balance			
								Debit		Credit	
Apr.	7		J1	250	00			250	00		

Total Points – 4

Account Title: *Miscellaneous Expense*   **Account No.** *520*

Date 20—		Explanation	Post. Ref.	Debit		Credit		Balance			
								Debit		Credit	

Total Points – 1

Account Title: *Salaries Expense*   **Account No.** *530*

Date 20—		Explanation	Post. Ref.	Debit		Credit		Balance			
								Debit		Credit	
Apr.	5		J1	600	00			600	00		
	11		J1	640	00			1240	00		

Total Points – 6

LIFEPAC TEST 4 (cont'd)

Teacher's Note: *Each item in this trial balance counts as* **one-half** *point, including each line of the heading, account titles, account numbers, amounts, correct totals and rulings (underlines). This problem has 54 individual items.* **Total Points – 27**

ACCOUNT TITLE	ACCT. NO.	DEBIT		CREDIT	
Burns Realty					
Trial Balance					
April 13, 20—					
Cash	*110*	*23545*	*00*		
Accounts Receivable	*120*				
Office Supplies	*130*	*975*	*00*		
Office Equipment	*140*	*16840*	*00*		
Automobile	*150*	*17500*	*00*		
Land	*160*	*62000*	*00*		
Building	*170*	*110000*	*00*		
Accounts Payable	*210*			*2740*	*00*
Mortgage Payable	*220*			*139000*	*00*
Robert Burns, Capital	*310*			*83000*	*00*
Robert Burns, Drawing	*320*	*1500*	*00*		
Appraisal Fees	*410*			*210*	*00*
Commissions	*420*			*8900*	*00*
Advertising Expense	*510*	*250*	*00*		
Miscellaneous Expense	*520*				
Salaries Expense	*530*	*1240*	*00*		
Totals		*233850*	*00*	*233850*	*00*

Journal	58 points
Ledger	89 points
Trial Balance	27 points
Total	174 points

LIFEPAC TEST 5

PART I

Teacher's Note: Each answer is worth 1 point. ***Total Points – 40***

1.	F		26.	a
2.	T		27.	b
3.	F		28.	c
4.	T		29.	c
5.	T		30.	a
6.	F		31.	b
7.	F		32.	c
8.	T		33.	d
9.	T		34.	b
10.	F		35.	a
11.	T		36.	c
12.	F		37.	d
13.	T		38.	b
14.	T		39.	c
15.	T		40.	b
16.	T			
17.	T			
18.	F			
19.	T			
20.	T			
21.	T			
22.	T			
23.	F			
24.	F			
25.	T			

PART II

Teacher's Note: Each item in the worksheet on the following page counts as **one point**, *including each line of the heading. All account titles, amounts, adjustments and rulings count as single items.* ***Total Points – 73***

Worksheet for LIFEPAC Test Exercise 41

Craft Shop

Worksheet

For the Month Ended April 30, 20—

ACCOUNT NAME	TRIAL BALANCE DEBIT	TRIAL BALANCE CREDIT	ADJUSTMENTS DEBIT	ADJUSTMENTS CREDIT	INCOME STATEMENT DEBIT	INCOME STATEMENT CREDIT	BALANCE SHEET DEBIT	BALANCE SHEET CREDIT
Cash	12454 00						12454 00	
Petty Cash	300 00						300 00	
Supplies – Office	2950 00			(a)1849 00			1101 00	
Prepaid Insurance	3800 00			(b)1400 00			2400 00	
Jones Office Supply		1771 00						1771 00
Craft Supply, Inc.		1660 00						1660 00
Jane Smith, Capital		13099 00						13099 00
Jane Smith, Drawing	1560 00						1560 00	
Sales		8834 00				8834 00		
Advertising Expense	1775 00				1775 00			
Insurance Expense			(b)1400 00		1400 00			
Miscellaneous Expense	615 00				615 00			
Rent Expense	1000 00				1000 00			
Repair Expense	885 00				885 00			
Supplies Expense – Office			(a)1849 00		1849 00			
Utilities Expense	25 00				25 00			
Totals	25364 00	25364 00	3249 00	3249 00	7549 00	8834 00	17815 00	16530 00
Net Income					1285 00			1285 00
					8834 00	8834 00	17815 00	17815 00

LIFEPAC TEST 6

PART I

Teacher's Note: Each answer is worth 1 point. **Total Points – 35**

1. T	24. b
2. F	25. a
3. T	26. c
4. T	27. c
5. F	28. d
6. F	29. c
7. F	30. b
8. T	31. d
9. T	32. a
10. T	33. a
11. F	34. a
12. T	35. c
13. T	
14. T	
15. T	
16. a	
17. c	
18. d	
19. b	
20. a	
21. c	
22. c	
23. a	

LIFEPAC TEST 6 (cont'd)

PART II

*Teacher's Note: Each item in the form below counts as **one point**, including each line of the heading. All account titles, amounts and rulings count as single items.* **Total Points – 28**

The Hartman Company					
Income Statement					
For the Month Ended November 30, 20—					
Revenue:					
Commissions				5200	00
Expenses:					
Advertising Expense	290	00			
Insurance Expense	500	00			
Miscellaneous Expense	480	00			
Rent Expense	1800	00			
Supplies Expense – Office	560	00			
Supplies Expense – Store	440	00			
Utilities Expense	340	00			
Total Expenses				4410	00
Net Income				790	00

*Teacher's Note: Each item in the form below counts as **one point**, including each line of the heading. All account titles, amounts and rulings count as single items.* **Total Points – 21**

The Hartman Company					
Statement of Owner's Equity					
For the Month Ended November 30, 20—					
Capital, November 1, 20—				8910	00
Add: Additional Investment	1500	00			
Net Income	790	00			
Net Increase in Capital				2290	00
Total				11200	00
Less: Withdrawals				950	00
Thomas Hartman, Capital, November 30, 20—				10250	00

LIFEPAC TEST 6 (cont'd)

*Teacher's Note: Each item in the form below counts as **one point**, including each line of the heading. All account titles, amounts, rulings and blank divider lines after double rulings count as single items.* **Total Points – 35**

The Hartman Company				
Balance Sheet				
November 30, 20—				
Assets				
Cash	3900	00		
Petty Cash	300	00		
Office Supplies	2700	00		
Store Supplies	3700	00		
Prepaid Insurance	1400	00		
Total Assets			12000	00
Liabilities				
Black's Insurance Co.	1100	00		
Staples Office Supply	650	00		
Total Liabilities			1750	00
Owner's Equity				
Thomas Hartman, Capital			10250	00
Total Liabilities and Owner's Equity			12000	00

True/False & Multiple Choice	35 points
Income Statement	28 points
Statement of Owner's Equity	21 points
Balance Sheet	35 points
Total Points	119 points

LIFEPAC TEST 7

PART I

Teacher's Note: *Each answer is worth 1 point.* ***Total Points – 40***

1.	F	21.	b
2.	F	22.	c
3.	T	23.	b
4.	T	24.	a
5.	T	25.	d
6.	T	26.	b
7.	F	27.	c
8.	F	28.	o
9.	F	29.	a
10.	F	30.	m
11.	a	31.	i
12.	c	32.	k
13.	a	33.	n
14.	c	34.	c
15.	d	35.	e
16.	a	36.	j
17.	b	37.	b
18.	d	38.	l
19.	d	39.	f
20.	a	40.	d

LIFEPAC TEST 7 (cont'd)

PART II

41. **Teacher's Note:** *Each answer below counts for* **one** *point. This problem has 45 answers.*
Total Points – 45

Account Title	Account adjusted from adjusting entries?		Account closed during closing procedure?		Account appears on the post-closing trial balance?	
	YES	NO	YES	NO	YES	NO
Cash		X		X	X	
Office Max		X		X	X	
Owner's Capital		X		X	X	
Owner's Drawing		X	X			X
Sales		X	X			X
Advertising Expense		X	X			X
Insurance Expense	X		X			X
Prepaid Insurance	X			X	X	
Rent Expense		X	X			X
Supplies	X			X	X	
Supplies Expense	X		X			X
Utilities Expense		X	X			X
Commissions		X	X			X
Petty Cash		X		X	X	
Mortgage Payable		X		X	X	

LIFEPAC TEST 7 (cont'd)

Teacher's Note: *Each item in the journal below counts as **one** point, including the page number, the year, the month and the day of the month. All headings, account titles and amounts count as single items. This problem has 45 individual items.* **Total Points – 45**

JOURNAL							Page	2

Date 20—		Account Title and Explanation	Doc No.	Post. Ref.	General Debit		General Credit	
		Adjusting Entries						
Sept.	30	*Supplies Expense*			1341	00		
		Supplies					1341	00
	30	*Insurance Expense*			330	00		
		Prepaid Insurance					330	00
		Closing Entries						
	30	*Sales*			4327	00		
		Income Summary					4327	00
	30	*Income Summary*			2427	00		
		Advertising Expense					86	00
		Insurance Expense					330	00
		Miscellaneous Expense					95	00
		Rent Expense					450	00
		Supplies Expense					1341	00
		Utilities Expense					125	00
	30	*Income Summary*			1900	00		
		Jan Davis, Capital					1900	00
	30	*Jan Davis, Capital*			500	00		
		Jan Davis, Drawing					500	00

True/False, Multiple Choice & Matching	40 points	
Chart	45 points	
Journal	45 points	
Total Points	130 points	

LIFEPAC TEST 8

Teacher's Note: *Each answer is worth 1 point.* **Total Points – 42**

1.	T		22.	a
2.	T		23.	b
3.	F		24.	b
4.	T		25.	a
5.	T		26.	c
6.	F		27.	a
7.	T		28.	b
8.	F		29.	c
9.	T		30.	k
10.	T		31.	e
11.	T		32.	l
12.	T		33.	n
13.	T		34.	d
14.	F		35.	m
15.	F		36.	f
16.	T		37.	a
17.	F		38.	h
18.	T		39.	b
19.	F		40.	c
20.	c		41.	j
21.	b		42.	g

43. **Teacher's Note:** *Each answer is worth* **one-half** *point. There are 36 individual answers, including two rulings.* **Total Points – 18**

FUN-TIME NOVELTIES
Time Sheet for the Week Ended *June 25, 20—*

EMPLOYEE NAME	MON	TUES	WED	THURS	FRI	REGULAR HOURS	OVERTIME HOURS	REGULAR RATE	REGULAR EARNINGS	OVERTIME RATE	OVERTIME EARNINGS
Allen, Joseph	9	6	8.5	7	8	38.5		8.56	329.56		
Baxter, Tina	8	9.5	7	6	10	**40**	.5	9.15	**366.00**	**13.725**	**6.86**
Charles, Henry	10	8	7	9	8	**40**	2	9.35	**374.00**	**14.025**	**28.05**
Day, Nora	7	9	9	10	7	**40**	2	8.85	**354.00**	**13.275**	**26.55**
Fry, Thomas	8	8	9	10	6	**40**	1	7.95	**318.00**	**11.925**	**11.93**
George, Marcia	7	9.5	10	6	9	**40**	1.5	8.10	**324.00**	**12.15**	**18.23**
Howe, Greg	8	6	9	10	7	**40**		7.89	**315.60**		
Jones, Melvin	10	8	9	7	7	**40**	1	9.25	**370.00**	**13.875**	**13.88**
									2751.16		105.50

44. **Teacher's Note:** *Each answer is worth* **one-half** *point. There are 62 individual answers, including the ruling.* **Total Points – 31**

PAYROLL REGISTER for the Weekly Payroll Period Ended   June 25, 20—

NO.	EMPLOYEE DATA			EARNINGS			DEDUCTIONS					NET PAY
	NAME	MARITAL STATUS	EXEMP.	REGULAR	OVERTIME	TOTAL	FEDERAL INCOME TAX	FICA	HEALTH INSURANCE	OTHER	TOTAL DEDUCTIONS	AMOUNT
1	Allen, Joseph	M	2	329 56		329 56	14 00	25 21			39 21	290 35
2	Baxter, Tina	M	3	366 00	6 86	372 86	13 00	28 52			41 52	331 34
3	Charles, Henry	M	1	374 00	28 05	402 05	34 00	30 76			64 76	337 29
4	Day, Nora	M	4	354 00	26 55	380 55	7 00	29 11			36 11	344 44
5	Fry, Thomas	M	2	318 00	11 93	329 93	14 00	25 24			39 24	290 69
6	George, Marcia	M	3	324 00	18 23	342 23	9 00	26 18			35 18	307 05
7	Howe, Greg	M	1	315 60		315 60	21 00	24 14			45 14	270 46
8	Jones, Melvin	M	2	370 00	13 88	383 88	23 00	29 37			52 37	331 51
	Totals			2751 16	105 50	2856 66	135 00	218 53			353 53	2503 13

True/False & Multiple Choice   42 points
Time Sheet   18 points
Payroll Register   31 points
Total Points   91 points

LIFEPAC TEST 9

1.	T	27.	c
2.	F	28.	a
3.	F	29.	b
4.	T	30.	c
5.	F	31.	d
6.	T	32.	b
7.	T	33.	a
8.	T	34.	c
9.	T	35.	d
10.	F	36.	c
11.	T	37.	a
12.	T	38.	c
13.	T	39.	b
14.	F	40.	c
15.	T	41.	k
16.	c	42.	j
17.	b	43.	g
18.	c	44.	f
19.	b	45.	c
20.	a	46.	d
21.	a	47.	b
22.	b	48.	e
23.	b	49.	h
24.	c	50.	i
25.	d	51.	a
26.	d		

LIFEPAC TEST 9 (cont'd)

Date 20—		Account Title and Explanation	Doc No.	Post. Ref.	General Debit		General Credit	
Mar.	15	*Salary Expense*			6270	00		
		Employee Income Tax Pay.					694	00
		FICA Tax Payable					388	74
		Medicare Tax Payable					90	92
		U. S. Savings Bonds Payable					100	00
		Cash	Ck260				4996	34
	15	*Payroll Taxes Expense*			868	40		
		FICA Tax Payable					388	74
		Medicare Tax Payable					90	92
		Unempl. Tax Pay. – Federal					50	16
		Unempl. Tax Pay. – State	M4				338	58
	31	*Salary Expense*			6982	00		
		Employee Income Tax Pay.					797	00
		FICA Tax Payable					432	88
		Medicare Tax Payable					101	24
		U. S. Savings Bonds Payable					75	00
		Cash	Ck290				5575	88
	31	*Payroll Taxes Expense*			967	01		
		FICA Tax Payable					432	88
		Medicare Tax Payable					101	24
		Unempl. Tax Pay. – Federal					55	86
		Unempl. Tax Pay. – State	M7				377	03

JOURNAL — Page 3

Payroll Tax Summary Sheet March 15, 20–   *Memo #4*

	Debit	Credit
Payroll Taxes Expense	$868.40	
FICA Tax Payable		338.74
Medicare Tax Payable		90.92
Unemployment Tax Payable – Federal		50.16
Unemployment Tax Payable – State		338.58

Payroll Tax Summary Sheet March 31, 20–   *Memo #7*

	Debit	Credit
Payroll Taxes Expense	$967.01	
FICA Tax Payable		432.88
Medicare Tax Payable		101.24
Unemployment Tax Payable – Federal		55.86
Unemployment Tax Payable – State		377.03

LIFEPAC TEST 10

1.	10,150.00		16.	1,800.00
2.	3,280.00		17.	111.60
3.	7,690.00		18.	Single
4.	1,303.60		19.	56,705.60
5.	445.00		20.	2,505.00
6.	229.50		21.	6,254.90
7.	14,350.50		22.	41,055.50
8.	March 30th		23.	5,615.00
9.	22,000.00		24.	21,905.00
10.	0		25.	38,505.50
11.	23,500.00		26.	7,754.90
12.	2,030.00		27.	27,204.90
13.	1,600.00		28.	38,505.50
14.	148.20		29.	15,650.10
15.	1		30.	11,300.60